G000292513

VB
FOR
DUMMIES®

Quick Reference

by Paul Litwin

IDG
BOOKS
WORLDWIDE

IDG Books Worldwide, Inc.
An International Data Group Company

Foster City, CA ✦ Chicago, IL ✦ Indianapolis, IN ✦ Southlake, TX

VBA For Dummies® Quick Reference

Published by
IDG Books Worldwide, Inc.
An International Data Group Company
919 E. Hillsdale Blvd.
Suite 400
Foster City, CA 94404
www.idgbooks.com (IDG Books Worldwide Web site)
www.dummies.com (Dummies Press Web site)

Copyright © 1997 IDG Books Worldwide, Inc. All rights reserved. No part of this book, including interior design, cover design, and icons, may be reproduced or transmitted in any form, by any means (electronic, photocopying, recording, or otherwise) without the prior written permission of the publisher.

Library of Congress Catalog Card No.: 97-73304

ISBN: 0-7645-0250-6

Printed in the United States of America

10 9 8 7 6 5 4 3 2 1

1A/SV/QX/ZX/IN

Distributed in the United States by IDG Books Worldwide, Inc.

Distributed by Macmillan Canada for Canada; by Transworld Publishers Limited in the United Kingdom; by IDG Norge Books for Norway; by IDG Sweden Books for Sweden; by Woodslane Pty. Ltd. for Australia; by Woodslane Enterprises Ltd. for New Zealand; by Longman Singapore Publishers Ltd. for Singapore, Malaysia, Thailand, and Indonesia; by Simron Pty. Ltd. for South Africa; by Toppan Company Ltd. for Japan; by Distribuidora Cuspide for Argentina; by Livraria Cultura for Brazil; by Ediciencia S.A. for Ecuador; by Addison-Wesley Publishing Company for Korea; by Ediciones ZETA S.C.R. Ltda. for Peru; by WS Computer Publishing Corporation, Inc., for the Philippines; by Unalis Corporation for Taiwan; by Contemporanea de Ediciones for Venezuela; by Computer Book & Magazine Store for Puerto Rico; by Express Computer Distributors for the Caribbean and West Indies. Authorized Sales Agent: Anthony Rudkin Associates for the Middle East and North Africa.

For general information on IDG Books Worldwide's books in the U.S., please call our Consumer Customer Service department at 800-762-2974. For reseller information, including discounts and premium sales, please call our Reseller Customer Service department at 800-434-3422.

For information on where to purchase IDG Books Worldwide's books outside the U.S., please contact our International Sales department at 415-655-3200 or fax 415-655-3295.

For information on foreign language translations, please contact our Foreign & Subsidiary Rights department at 415-655-3021 or fax 415-655-3281.

For sales inquiries and special prices for bulk quantities, please contact our Sales department at 415-655-3200 or write to the address above.

For information on using IDG Books Worldwide's books in the classroom or for ordering examination copies, please contact our Educational Sales department at 800-434-2086 or fax 817-251-8174.

For press review copies, author interviews, or other publicity information, please contact our Public Relations department at 415-655-3000 or fax 415-655-3299.

For authorization to photocopy items for corporate, personal, or educational use, please contact Copyright Clearance Center, 222 Rosewood Drive, Danvers, MA 01923, or fax 508-750-4470.

LIMIT OF LIABILITY/DISCLAIMER OF WARRANTY: AUTHOR AND PUBLISHER HAVE USED THEIR BEST EFFORTS IN PREPARING THIS BOOK. IDG BOOKS WORLDWIDE, INC., AND AUTHOR MAKE NO REPRESENTATIONS OR WARRANTIES WITH RESPECT TO THE ACCURACY OR COMPLETENESS OF THE CONTENTS OF THIS BOOK AND SPECIFICALLY DISCLAIM ANY IMPLIED WARRANTIES OF MERCHANTABILITY OR FITNESS FOR A PARTICULAR PURPOSE. THERE ARE NO WARRANTIES WHICH EXTEND BEYOND THE DESCRIPTIONS CONTAINED IN THIS PARAGRAPH. NO WARRANTY MAY BE CREATED OR EXTENDED BY SALES REPRESENTATIVES OR WRITTEN SALES MATERIALS. THE ACCURACY AND COMPLETENESS OF THE INFORMATION PROVIDED HEREIN AND THE OPINIONS STATED HEREIN ARE NOT GUARANTEED OR WARRANTED TO PRODUCE ANY PARTICULAR RESULTS, AND THE ADVICE AND STRATEGIES CONTAINED HEREIN MAY NOT BE SUITABLE FOR EVERY INDI-VIDUAL. NEITHER IDG BOOKS WORLDWIDE, INC., NOR AUTHOR SHALL BE LIABLE FOR ANY LOSS OF PROFIT OR ANY OTHER COMMERCIAL DAMAGES, INCLUDING BUT NOT LIMITED TO SPECIAL, INCIDENTAL, CONSE-QUENTIAL, OR OTHER DAMAGES.

Trademarks: All brand names and product names used in this book are trade names, service marks, trademarks, or registered trademarks of their respective owners. IDG Books Worldwide is not associated with any product or vendor mentioned in this book.

is a trademark under exclusive
license to IDG Books Worldwide, Inc.,
from International Data Group, Inc.

About the Author

Paul Litwin is an internationally recognized speaker, trainer, author, and developer. Paul is a senior consultant and principal at MCW Technologies focusing on application development employing Access, Visual Basic, Microsoft Office, SQL Server, and Internet technologies. He has written numerous articles for publications, including *Smart Access, Visual Basic Programmer's Journal,* and *PC World.* He also wrote the Jet Engine White Paper for Microsoft. Paul has authored several books on Access 2 and Access 95, and recently co-authored a book on Access 97. He trains developers for Application Developers Training Company and is a regular speaker at conferences, including Tech*Ed, Windows Solutions, Windows Solutions Tokyo, DevDays, Access Teach, and VB Teach. Paul is also a Microsoft Access MVP (most valuable professional) specializing in helping users with Access and Internet integration problems. In what little spare time he has, Paul enjoys spending time with his family, running, and coaching his 10-year-old son's soccer team.

You can reach Paul at plitwin@mcwtech.com or http://www.mcwtech.com.

ABOUT IDG BOOKS WORLDWIDE

Welcome to the world of IDG Books Worldwide.

IDG Books Worldwide, Inc., is a subsidiary of International Data Group, the world's largest publisher of computer-related information and the leading global provider of information services on information technology. IDG was founded more than 25 years ago and now employs more than 8,500 people worldwide. IDG publishes more than 275 computer publications in over 75 countries (see listing below). More than 60 million people read one or more IDG publications each month.

Launched in 1990, IDG Books Worldwide is today the #1 publisher of best-selling computer books in the United States. We are proud to have received eight awards from the Computer Press Association in recognition of editorial excellence and three from *Computer Currents'* First Annual Readers' Choice Awards. Our best-selling ...For Dummies® series has more than 30 million copies in print with translations in 30 languages. IDG Books Worldwide, through a joint venture with IDG's Hi-Tech Beijing, became the first U.S. publisher to publish a computer book in the People's Republic of China. In record time, IDG Books Worldwide has become the first choice for millions of readers around the world who want to learn how to better manage their businesses.

Our mission is simple: Every one of our books is designed to bring extra value and skill-building instructions to the reader. Our books are written by experts who understand and care about our readers. The knowledge base of our editorial staff comes from years of experience in publishing, education, and journalism — experience we use to produce books for the '90s. In short, we care about books, so we attract the best people. We devote special attention to details such as audience, interior design, use of icons, and illustrations. And because we use an efficient process of authoring, editing, and desktop publishing our books electronically, we can spend more time ensuring superior content and spend less time on the technicalities of making books.

You can count on our commitment to deliver high-quality books at competitive prices on topics you want to read about. At IDG Books Worldwide, we continue in the IDG tradition of delivering quality for more than 25 years. You'll find no better book on a subject than one from IDG Books Worldwide.

IDG BOOKS WORLDWIDE

John Kilcullen
CEO
IDG Books Worldwide, Inc.

Steven Berkowitz
President and Publisher
IDG Books Worldwide, Inc.

Eighth Annual Computer Press Awards ≥ 1992

Ninth Annual Computer Press Awards ≥ 1993

Tenth Annual Computer Press Awards ≥ 1994

Eleventh Annual Computer Press Awards ≥ 1995

IDG Books Worldwide, Inc., is a subsidiary of International Data Group, the world's largest publisher of computer-related information and the leading global provider of information services on information technology. International Data Group publishes over 275 computer publications in over 75 countries. Sixty million people read one or more International Data Group publications each month. International Data Group's publications include: **ARGENTINA:** Buyer's Guide, Computerworld Argentina, PC World Argentina; **AUSTRALIA:** Australian Macworld, Australian PC World, Australian Reseller News, Computerworld, IT Casebook, Network World, Publish, Webmaster; **AUSTRIA:** Computerwelt Österreich, Networks Austria, PC Tip Austria; **BANGLADESH:** PC World Bangladesh; **BELARUS:** PC World Belarus; **BELGIUM:** Data News; **BRAZIL:** Annuário de Informática, Computerworld, Connections, Macworld, PC Player, PC World, Publish, Reseller News, Supergamepower; **BULGARIA:** Computerworld Bulgaria, Network World Bulgaria, PC & MacWorld Bulgaria; **CANADA:** CIO Canada, Client/Server World, ComputerWorld Canada, InfoWorld Canada, NetworkWorld Canada, WebWorld; **CHILE:** Computerworld Chile, PC World Chile; **COLOMBIA:** Computerworld Colombia, PC World Colombia; **COSTA RICA:** PC World Centro America; **THE CZECH AND SLOVAK REPUBLICS:** Computerworld Czechoslovakia, Macworld Czech Republic, PC World Czechoslovakia; **DENMARK:** Communications World Danmark, Computerworld Danmark, Macworld Danmark, PC World Danmark, Techworld Denmark; **DOMINICAN REPUBLIC:** PC World Republica Dominicana; **ECUADOR:** PC World Ecuador; **EGYPT:** Computerworld Middle East, PC World Middle East; **EL SALVADOR:** PC World Centro America; **FINLAND:** MikroPC, Tietoverkko, Tietoviikko; **FRANCE:** Distributique, Hebdo, Info PC, Le Monde Informatique, Macworld, Reseaux & Telecoms, WebMaster France; **GERMANY:** Computer Partner, Computerwoche, Computerwoche Extra, Computerwoche FOCUS, Global Online, Macwelt, PC Welt; **GREECE:** Amiga Computing, GamePro Greece, Multimedia World; **GUATEMALA:** PC World Centro America; **HONDURAS:** PC World Centro America; **HONG KONG:** Computerworld Hong Kong, PC World Hong Kong, Publish in Asia; **HUNGARY:** ABCD CD-ROM, Computerworld Szamitastechnika, Internetto online Magazine, PC World Hungary, PC-X Magazin Hungary; **ICELAND:** Tolvuheimur PC World Island; **INDIA:** Information Communications World, Information Systems Computerworld, PC World India, Publish in Asia; **INDONESIA:** InfoKomputer PC World, Komputek Computerworld, Publish in Asia; **IRELAND:** ComputerScope, PC Live!; **ISRAEL:** Macworld Israel, People & Computers/Computerworld; **ITALY:** Computerworld Italia, Macworld Italia, Networking Italia, PC World Italia; **JAPAN:** DTP World, Macworld Japan, Nikkei Personal Computing, OS/2 World Japan, SunWorld Japan, Windows NT World, Windows World Japan; **KENYA:** PC World East African; **KOREA:** Hi-Tech Information, Macworld Korea, PC World Korea; **MACEDONIA:** PC World Macedonia; **MALAYSIA:** Computerworld Malaysia, PC World Malaysia, Publish in Asia; **MALTA:** PC World Malta; **MEXICO:** Computerworld Mexico, PC World Mexico; **MYANMAR:** PC World Myanmar; **NETHERLANDS:** Computer! Totaal, LAN Internetworking Magazine, LAN World Buyers Guide, Macworld Netherlands, Net, WebWereld; **NEW ZEALAND:** Absolute Beginners Guide and Plain & Simple Series, Computer Buyer, Computer Industry Directory, Computerworld New Zealand, MTB, Network World, PC World New Zealand; **NICARAGUA:** PC World Centro America; **NORWAY:** Computerworld Norge, CW Rapport, Datamagasinet, Financial Rapport, Kursguide Norge, Macworld Norge, Multimediaworld Norge, PC World Ekspress Norge, PC World Nettverk, PC World Norge, PC World ProduktGuide Norge; **PAKISTAN:** Computerworld Pakistan; **PANAMA:** PC World Panama; **PEOPLE'S REPUBLIC OF CHINA:** China Computer Users, China Computerworld, China InfoWorld, China Telecom World Weekly, Computer & Communication, Electronic Design China, Electronics Today, Electronics Weekly, Game Software, PC World China, Popular Computer Week, Software Weekly, Software World, Telecom World; **PERU:** Computerworld Peru, PC World Profesional Peru, PC World SoHo Peru; **PHILIPPINES:** Click!, Computerworld Philippines, PC World Philippines, Publish in Asia; **POLAND:** Computerworld Poland, Computerworld Special Report Poland, Cyber, Macworld Poland, Networld Poland, PC World Komputer; **PORTUGAL:** Cerebro/PC World, Computerworld/Correio Informatico, Dealer World Portugal, Mac*In/PC*In Portugal, Multimedia World; **PUERTO RICO:** Computerworld Puerto Rico; **ROMANIA:** Computerworld Romania, PC World Romania, Telecom Romania; **RUSSIA:** Computerworld Russia, Mir PK, Publish, Seti; **SINGAPORE:** Computerworld Singapore, PC World Singapore, Publish in Asia; **SLOVENIA:** Monitor; **SOUTH AFRICA:** Computing SA, Network World SA, Software World SA; **SPAIN:** Communicaciones World España, Computerworld España, Dealer World España, Macworld España, PC World España; **SRI LANKA:** Infolink PC World; **SWEDEN:** CAP&Design, Computer Sweden, Corporate Computing Sweden, Internetworld Sweden, it.branschen, Macworld Sweden, MaxiData Sweden, MikroDatorn, Nätverk & Kommunikation, PC World Sweden, PCaktiv, Windows World Sweden; **SWITZERLAND:** Computerworld Schweiz, Macworld Schweiz, PCtip; **TAIWAN:** Computerworld Taiwan, Macworld Taiwan, NEW ViSiON/Publish, PC World Taiwan, Windows World Taiwan; **THAILAND:** Publish in Asia, Thai Computerworld; **TURKEY:** Computerworld Turkiye, Macworld Turkiye, Network World Turkiye, PC World Turkiye; **UKRAINE:** Computerworld Kiev, Multimedia World Ukraine, PC World Ukraine; **UNITED KINGDOM:** Acorn User UK, Amiga Action UK, Amiga Computing UK, Apple Talk UK, Computing, Macworld, Parents and Computers UK, PC Advisor, PC Home, PSX Pro, The WEB; **UNITED STATES:** Cable in the Classroom, CIO Magazine, Computerworld, DOS World, Federal Computer Week, GamePro Magazine, InfoWorld, I-Way, Macworld, Network World, PC Games, PC World, Publish, Video Event, THE WEB Magazine, and WebMaster; online webzines: JavaWorld, NetscapeWorld, and SunWorld Online; **URUGUAY:** InfoWorld Uruguay; **VENEZUELA:** Computerworld Venezuela, PC World Venezuela; and **VIETNAM:** PC World Vietnam.
3/24/97

Dedication

In loving memory of my wife Alicia's parents, Al Comstock and Margaret Brown Comstock, who always treated me as if I were their own son.

Author's Acknowledgments

I'd like to thank the many fine people at IDG Books who helped make this book a reality, including my acquisitions editor, Jill Pisoni, and project editor, Rev Mengle. The technical accuracy of this book was improved greatly by the diligent work of the book's technical editor, David Shank.

Thanks also go to my business associate and friend, Ken Getz, who encouraged me to write this book and who took the time to look over the first few chapters.

Of course, without the support of my wife, Alicia, and son, Geoffrey, as well as the continued support of my parents and the rest of my family, this book wouldn't have been possible.

Publisher's Acknowledgments

We're proud of this book; please send us your comments about it by using the IDG Books Worldwide Registration Card at the back of the book or by e-mailing us at feedback/dummies@idgbooks.com. Some of the people who helped bring this book to market include the following:

Acquisitions, Development, and Editorial

Project Editor: Rev Mengle

Senior Acquisitions Editor: Jill Pisoni

Product Development Director: Mary Bednarek

Copy Editor: Patricia Pan

Technical Editor: David Shank, Microsoft Corp.

Editorial Manager: Colleen Rainsberger

Editorial Assistant: Darren Meiss

Production

Project Coordinator: Debbie Stailey

Layout and Graphics: Lou Boudreau, Elizabeth Cárdenas-Nelson, Pamela Emanoil, Kate Snell

Proofreaders: Nancy L. Reinhardt, Christine Berman, Robert Springer

Indexer: Sharon Duffy

Special Help

Stephanie Koutek, Proof Editor
Donna Love, Editorial Assistant

General and Administrative

IDG Books Worldwide, Inc.: John Kilcullen, CEO; Steven Berkowitz, President and Publisher

IDG Books Technology Publishing: Brenda McLaughlin, Senior Vice President and Group Publisher

Dummies Technology Press and Dummies Editorial: Diane Graves Steele, Vice President and Associate Publisher; Judith A. Taylor, Product Marketing Manager; Kristin A. Cocks, Editorial Director

Dummies Trade Press: Kathleen A. Welton, Vice President and Publisher

IDG Books Production for Dummies Press: Beth Jenkins, Production Director; Cindy L. Phipps, Manager of Project Coordination, Production Proofreading, and Indexing; Kathie S. Schutte, Supervisor of Page Layout; Shelley Lea, Supervisor of Graphics and Design; Debbie J. Gates, Production Systems Specialist; Tony Augsburger, Supervisor of Reprints and Bluelines; Leslie Popplewell, Media Archive Coordinator

Dummies Packaging and Book Design: Patti Sandez, Packaging Specialist; Lance Kayser, Packaging Assistant; Kavish + Kavish, Cover Design

◆

The publisher would like to give special thanks to Patrick J. McGovern, without whom this book would not have been possible.

◆

Table of Contents

Part VI: Debugging and Error Handling 59

Part VII: Files, Input, and Output 67

Part X: Miscellaneous 123

Part XI: Procedures 139

Part XII: String Manipulation 151

How to Use This Book

Visual Basic for Applications (hereafter called VBA for short) has finally arrived! It's been many, many years in the making, but, finally, Microsoft has delivered Office 97 with a single, consistent, powerful language pervading all its desktop applications. (Well, Microsoft Outlook actually uses VBScript — a subset of VBA — as its programming language, but it's close enough.) What's more, Microsoft has also licensed the VBA language to other vendors so VBA now appears in products such as Visio, Adobe Photoshop, Crystal Reports, and lots of other programs.

This book is for all you VBA programmers who want a quick way to look up information on the core VBA language. Yes, the info is probably somewhere there in online Help, but there are times when paper is better.

About This Book

This book is a quick reference for VBA *programmers*. It doesn't teach you how to program or how to use Microsoft Office. It isn't a step-by-step guide, nor is it for absolute beginners. If you need help getting started with Office, take a look at *Microsoft Office 97 For Windows For Dummies*, by Wallace Wang. If you want to start programming Microsoft Office using VBA, go out and get *Microsoft Office 97 Programming with VBA For Dummies*, by Karen Jaskolka and Mike Gilbert. IDG Books Worldwide, Inc. publishes both books.

Microsoft no longer includes a language reference with Office. Other VBA vendors are likely to do the same. True, some sort of language reference is always there in online Help, but some programmers — including me — still like a paper-based quick reference guide to help them in their time of need. I hope this text fills that need. In addition, to an extensive keyword reference to the core VBA language, I also include a bit of help on using the VBA integrated development environment (IDE) and a bunch of diagrams of the Microsoft Office 97 object models.

The most important element of this book is that it puts the information you need to effectively program in VBA at your fingertips. Most of this information is available elsewhere — after all this isn't rocket science — but nowhere as conveniently packaged as you find here. In fact, I wrote this book partly so *I* could have a paper-based quick reference when *I* program in VBA. I hope you like it too.

What's Not Here

Each VBA host product (such as Microsoft Access or Visio) adds product-specific syntax to its implementation of VBA. You don't find those product-specific extensions here: This book includes only the keywords that all VBA products share, the so-called *core VBA language*.

While I do include diagrams of the Microsoft Office 97 object models, I simply don't have the room for other products' object models, not do I have room to list the properties, methods, and events for each Office 97 product. No can do, amigo. So while the object models should be enough to get you started, you have to depend on other sources — an excellent one being the aforementioned *Microsoft Office 97 Programming with VBA For Dummies* — to help you on these other parts of VBA programming. You may also find help from the online help facility of your VBA host product or the new IntelliSense features that automatically drop down a list of available properties and methods for objects as you type. You find out more about IntelliSense features in Part I.

A Word about VBA's Past and Future

You've probably been hearing lots about Java, but there are tons more people programming with VBA and its sister languages, Visual Basic and VBScript, than there are Java programmers. In fact, VBA is now part of, or soon will be part of, more than 50 products on a variety of platforms. Why is this? Because VBA, unlike Java, is very easy to learn and use. And VBA is definitely not a member of the language-of-the-week club. (VBA's parent language, BASIC, was invented in 1964 at Dartmouth College.) So fear not. VBA, unlike some other fly-by-night languages — and I'm not mentioning any names — is here to stay!

What Are All These Parts?

This book is divided into a bunch of distinct parts; they're sort of like chapters but with a different name:

Part I: Getting to Know VBA and the VBA IDE. This part orients you to the VBA language and the VBA integrated development environment (IDE) — that's computerese for that place where you enter, edit, and debug your VBA code. In this part, you find among other things, the VBA IDE's keyboard shortcuts.

Part II: Application Integration. This part and the next 12 parts make up the bulk of the book, covering the syntax of the core VBA language. Part II discusses the VBA keywords used to control other applications.

Part III: Arrays and Collections. This part covers the VBA keywords you use to manipulate arrays and collections.

Part IV: Conversion. This part covers conversion keywords, including all those functions you need to use to convert variables from one data type to another.

Part V: Date and Time Manipulation. Here, you find those functions used for date and time manipulation. I'm not talking relativity and quantum physics here; instead, you find out about less exciting functions like the function that returns the current date and time.

Part VI: Debugging and Error Handling. This part tackles error handling. What? You say you don't make no stinkin' errors? Guess again.

Part VII: Files, Input, and Output. In this part, you find elements of the language that you use for file manipulation and basic file input and output. Think of it as the "fun with files" part.

Part VIII: Looping and Branching. This part covers looping and branching. If you can't remember if it's "While Do" or "Do While," this is the place for you.

Part IX: Mathematical and Financial Operations. In this part you find the VBA equivalents of the mathematical and financial calculators. And you thought VBA wasn't fun.

Part X: Miscellaneous. This part covers all those things that don't fit anywhere else — the so-called miscellaneous keywords. Here you find keywords on diverse topics such as reading and writing to the registry, sounding a tone, and compiler directives. Isn't miscellaneous a weird word?

Part XI: Procedures. It's time to get procedural. Here you find keywords you can use to create and call procedures.

Part XII: String Manipulation. This part covers manipulating strings — that's programming strings, not the things that cats play with.

Part XIII: User Forms. This part covers VBA's forms, which you can display and manipulate with the keywords found in this part.

Part XIV: Variables and Constants. This part concerns itself with variables and constants. These are the things that vary and stay constant, respectively. Somehow, I bet you knew that already.

Part XV: Microsoft Office 97 Object Models. Here I present a bunch of cheat sheets for working with the Microsoft Office 97 Object Models. If you plan to have your VBA code interact with the Office 97 objects, then you may want to check out these swell diagrams. They double as "maps of the stars" — just kidding.

Icons, Schmicons

Scattered throughout the text you may run into some icons. No, I'm not talking about little pieces of religious art — these icons are small, goofy-looking pictures that I inserted to help keep the non-coffee drinkers awake. Here's a list of what's what in the iconic world:

This means to watch out. If you don't heed this warning, you may cause great harm to your code, computer, or love life.

This signifies an extra special little tip, just because I like you. Isn't that special?

Watch out, something funky is about to happen. (Do you hear the disco music playing?) The action won't damage anything, but it may surprise you.

You find this icon next to some advice that saves you a significant amount of time or is an important aspect of becoming a better, more efficient VBA programmer. (Time for the *Go Speed Racer, Go!* music.)

How to Read the Keyword References

In Parts II though XIV, you find a quick reference to the core VBA language.

Remember: You don't find keywords here that are product-specific. I include only those elements of the language that are common to all VBA implementations.

Preceding the keyword definitions for each part is the *Keyword Summary* section. Here you find a list of tasks (under Task) arranged alphabetically by task, the keyword you use to accomplish this task (under Keyword) and the type of keyword (under Keyword Type). Thus, for example, if you're looking for a keyword that returns the length of a string, you would jump to Part XII (String Manipulation) and look under the *String Manipulation Keyword Summary* section. Here you'd learn that to "determine the length of a string" you need to use the Len function.

All of the language reference parts of the book follow the same format. A sample appears here:

ReverseIt (Function)

Description: Reverses the input string, returning the first character of the input string as the last character and the last character of the input string as the first character.

Syntax:

```
ReverseIt ( inputstring [, makeuppercase] )
```

Arguments	Description
inputstring	Any string.
makeuppercase	Optional. If True, ReverseIt also changes all characters to uppercase. Defaults to False.

Example:

```
varRev = ReverseIt( "garbage" ) '= egabrag
```

Notes: This keyword is a fictional VBA function; it doesn't really exist.

Let's dissect the ReverseIt function reference. (I hope it doesn't get too icky!)

First, the *heading* for the keyword lists the keyword followed by the type of keyword it is in parentheses. In this case, ReverseIt is the keyword, and its type is a function. The majority of keywords are either functions or statements. Occasionally, you find some other type of keyword such as a method, a property, or an operator.

Right under the heading for the keyword, you find the word *Description* followed by a brief description of the keyword. In this case, the description is "Reverses the input string, returning the first character of the input string as the last character and the last character of the input string as the first character." Notice that it talks about *returning* a value, which is typical for a function because functions always return a value.

The next section, titled *Syntax,* describes the syntax of the keyword in official syntaxese. This style is very similar to the style you find for keywords in the online help system. The syntax may look a bit weird, but it's important that you get used to this format for you to get the most of this quick reference. Keep in mind the following:

+ The keyword itself (in this example, `ReverseIt`) is set in bold type.

+ Any other verbatim text — text you must type literally — is set in regular type. In this example, other than the parentheses, there is no verbatim text.

+ Replaceable text — text you must replace with some other information — is set in *italics*. In this example, there are two replaceable elements, *inputstring* and *[makeuppercase]*.

+ Optional items — text that you don't have to include — are surrounded by brackets. Don't type the brackets! In this example, *makeuppercase* is optional.

Following the syntax, you find a list of all the *Arguments* from the syntax section with a brief description of each argument. Here are a couple things to consider when reading the list of arguments:

+ If the argument is optional, the description will begin with "Optional." If you don't see this word, the argument is mandatory.

+ For all optional arguments, you also find a mention of the default value — the value VBA uses if you don't include this argument.

Most keywords can be typed using either *positional* or *named* arguments. Most examples use positional arguments. However, the names you find in the arguments list correspond to the names you would use if you used named arguments.

For many readers, the *Example* section is the most important. This is where you find the syntax and parameters translated into seminormal usage. This information, when combined with the syntax and parameters information, tells you just about everything you may want to know about the particular keyword. I take extra care to make the example (or examples) something you can type without causing an error. (The example may, however, require you to define a variable first. In the preceding case, you'd have to first declare the `varRev` variable with a `Dim` statement before typing the example.) Often, as shown in these sample examples (can you say that six times fast?), you find a comment to the right of the example that tells you the return value of a function. In these examples, the comment tells you that `varRev` returns either `egabrag` or `EGABRAG`.

Finally, the *Notes* section tells you anything else you need to know about the function. In this example, you are told that `ReverseIt` is not a real VBA function. Sorry!

How to Read the Object Model Diagrams

In Part XV, you find the object models for 13 Microsoft Office components. The object models are schematic diagrams that help you to understand the relationships between objects of an application or component. Object models come in handy when you need to programmatically manipulate an object of your VBA host application. They also come in handy when you need to program some shared Office component, such as CommandBars, or when you want to use Automation to control another application.

At the beginning of Part XV, you find a key that describes each of the elements of the object model diagrams. The key tells you, for example, that one type of rectangle stands for a single object, whereas another stands for a collection of objects. See the beginning of Part XV for more details.

Where To Go from Here

This book, of course, is only a quick reference guide to the VBA language, and comes in real handy once you're fairly comfortable with the language and already understand your host application. And because this book is only a quick reference, it doesn't get into as many details as a regular ...*For Dummies* book. For more information about using Microsoft Office, you want to consult *Microsoft Office 97 For Dummies*. If, instead, you're looking for more information on programming Microsoft Office, pick up a copy of *Microsoft Office 97 Programming With VBA For Dummies*.

If your VBA host product is not part of Microsoft Office, these books won't be that useful. Check your local bookstore to see if a ...*For Dummies* book for your application exists.

Many products have magazines and newsletters that are chock full of information about the product. If you still have trouble finding enough information on your product, try firing up your Web browser and jumping to your host application's Web site (such as `http://www.visio.com`, `http://www.adobe.com`, or `http://www.img.seagatesoftware.com`) or searching for information about your favorite application on the Internet using a search engine such as Alta Vista (`http://www.altavista.digital.com`).

Part I

Getting to Know VBA and the VBA IDE

The VBA programming language is rich and powerful, just like its creator Bill Gates. Part I starts with an overview of VBA, where you learn what VBA is, where it sits in the Visual Basic animal kingdom, and how it fits into your host's ecosystem.

Next, you explore the VBA IDE — the place where you create your VBA applications. The VBA IDE does almost everything for you so you can concentrate on what you do best: browsing the Web for the latest *Dilbert* comic strip — er, I mean *coding*. A few years ago, you were lucky if your code editor included a big blank area and a menu with File⇨Save and Quit as its only choices. But you and other developers complained and said you wanted more. Well, Microsoft listened and delivered the Mercedes of code editors: VBA IDE.

The VBA IDE includes lots of cool features that make easy work out of entering, editing, debugging, and managing your code. One of the newest features, called IntelliSense (can you tell the marketing folks created this name?), practically writes your code for you. What more can you ask for? Part I helps you get the most out of the VBA IDE by telling you how to make it sit, roll over, and give you its paw — or at least the programming equivalents of these canine commands. So sit back — I said *sit!* — and let's begin.

In this part . . .

- ✔ Introducing VBA
- ✔ Understanding the layout of the VBA editor hosts
- ✔ Learning the menus
- ✔ Learning the keyboard shortcuts

A Brief Look at VBA

Visual Basic for Applications (VBA) is a rich, mature programming language that's a visual, object-based derivative of the original BASIC created at Dartmouth College in 1964 by John Kemeny and Thomas Kurtz. VBA is part of the family of languages from Microsoft that also includes Visual Basic and VBScript. Visual Basic is the mammal of the family — it's a general purpose programming environment for creating *stand-alone* applications. VBA, on the other hand, is the parasite of the family. As the "for Applications" part of its name implies VBA cannot stand alone; it can live only within a host application. Have no fear, though, VBA is a good parasite that has a symbiotic relationship with its host. The third member of the Visual Basic family, VBScript, is the bacterium of the family. VBScript is a "lean and mean" subset of VBA created for Internet application development.

Okay, that's it for the biology metaphors — at least for a while.

Before you can create a VBA application, you must first choose a VBA host in which you create your application. For example, you may choose Microsoft Excel for financial planning applications, Microsoft Access for database applications, Microsoft Word for word processing applications, or Visio for drawing applications. (***See also*** the Introduction for a list of additional VBA hosts.)

What can you do with VBA? Just about anything. While easy to learn and use, the VBA language packs powerful functionality. The core VBA language includes more than 200 keywords. VBA keywords exist for testing conditions; looping and branching; creating variables, arrays, and collections; manipulating numbers, strings, dates, and times; reading and writing information to files; making financial and trigonometric calculations; interacting with your host application's data and objects; and controlling other applications. In fact, there's very little the VBA language *can't* do.

So how do you go about creating a VBA application? Well, after you choose your host, it's time to call up the VBA IDE, which brings us to our next topic.

A Warm Welcome to the VBA IDE

Nice of you to visit. Why don't you stay a while? There's a whole lot lotta stuff going on in the VBA Integrated Development Environment (IDE), which is also sometimes known simply as the *VBA Editor*.

Project Explorer   Code windows

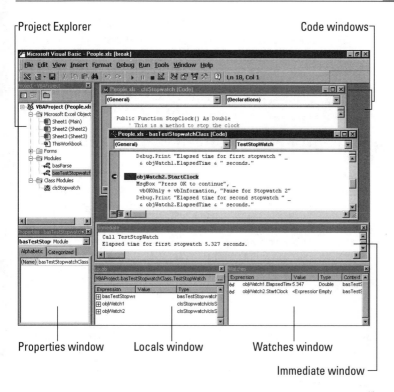

Properties window   Locals window   Watches window

Immediate window

You don't know how to start the VBA IDE? No problem, simply choose Tools➪Macro➪Visual Basic Editor or press Alt+F11. (Microsoft Access users: you need to choose View➪Code instead.)

The VBA IDE includes the following elements:

✦ **Project Explorer.** This is a hierarchical view of your project (which is another name for application).

✦ **Code window.** This is it — the place where you actually type your VBA code.

✦ **Properties window.** This is where you name (or rename) your modules. You also use this window for adjusting the properties of User Forms and their controls.

✦ **Immediate window.** This is where you test your VBA programs and evaluate single lines of VBA code. You can also send text to this window from your VBA programs.

✦ **Locals window.** When you test your VBA programs, you can use this handy-dandy window to look up the value of a variable or the property of an object.

◆ **Watches window.** Sometimes the locals window isn't enough. In these cases, you can define custom watch expressions that you can keep an eye on while your program runs.

◆ Microsoft Access isn't a full-fledged VBA IDE citizen. While the Access IDE fully implements the VBA language, its IDE is a bit different.

Getting Around the VBA IDE

Think of this section as a quick reference to all the VBA IDE commands. You find here the menu command and keyboard shortcut for just about anything you can do in the VBA editor.

Microsoft Access tries to be different. In the following sections, you find an asterisk next to any feature that's done differently in Access, as well as a separate entry for Access. If an item appears with two asterisks, however, that means there is no corresponding feature in Access.

Breakpoint shortcuts

You use these shortcuts to manage breakpoints in your code:

Feature Shortcut	Menu Command	Keyboard
Set or unset a breakpoint	Debug⇨Toggle Breakpoint	F9
Clear all breakpoints	Debug⇨Clear All Breakpoints	Ctrl+Shift+F9

Editing shortcuts

Use these shortcuts to edit your code:

Type	Feature	Menu Command	Keyboard Shortcut
Clipboarding	Copy the selection to the clipboard	Edit⇨Copy	Ctrl+C
	Cut the selection to the clipboard	Edit⇨Cut	Ctrl+X
	Delete the selected text without copying it to the clipboard*	Edit⇨Clear	Del
	Delete the selected text without copying it to the clipboard (Access)	Edit⇨Delete	Del

Type	Feature	Menu Command	Keyboard Shortcut
	Paste the contents of the clipboard at the location of the cursor	Edit⇨Paste	Ctrl+V
	Select all text in the module window	Edit⇨Select All	Ctrl+A
Indenting	Indent the selected text one tab stop	Edit⇨Indent	Tab
	Outdent the selected text one tab stop	Edit⇨Outdent	Shift+Tab
Bookmarking	Bookmark or unbookmark the current line*	Edit⇨Bookmarks⇨ Toggle Bookmark	*none*
	Bookmark or unbookmark the current line (Access)	Edit⇨Bookmarks⇨ Bookmark	*none*
	Go to the next bookmark	Edit⇨Bookmarks⇨ Next Bookmark	*none*
	Go to the prior bookmark	Edit⇨Bookmarks⇨ Previous Bookmark	*none*
	Clear all bookmarks	Edit⇨Bookmarks⇨ Clear All Bookmarks	*none*
Undoing	Undo the previous action	Edit⇨Undo	Ctrl+Z
	Redo the previous undone action	Edit⇨Redo	*none*

File operation shortcuts

Use the following shortcuts to do file stuff:

Type	Feature	Menu Command	Keyboard Shortcut
Starting	Starting the VBA IDE*	Tools⇨Macro⇨ Visual Basic Editor	Alt+F11
	Starting the VBA IDE (Access)	View⇨Code	*none*
Saving	Save the current project	File⇨Save *modulename*	Ctrl+S
Importing/ Exporting	Import a file*	File⇨Import file	Ctrl+M
	Import a file (Access)	File⇨ Get External Data⇨ Import	*none*
	Export a file*	File⇨Export File	Ctrl+E
	Export a file (Access)	File⇨Save As Text	*none*

(continued)

Type	Feature	Menu Command	Keyboard Shortcut
Deleting	Delete the current module*	File⇨Remove *modulename*	*none*
	Delete the current module (Access)	must exit IDE and select Edit⇨Delete	Del
Printing	Print the current module	File⇨Print	Ctrl+P
Closing	Close the IDE and return to host*	File⇨Close and Return to *host*	Alt+Q
	Close the IDE and return to host (Access)	File⇨Close	*none*
Inserting	Insert a new procedure	Insert⇨Procedure	*none*
	Insert a new standard module	Insert⇨Module	*none*
	Insert a new class module	Insert⇨Class Module	*none*
	Insert a new user form**	Insert⇨UserForm	*none*
	Insert a file into the current module	Insert⇨File	*none*

Help shortcuts

Here's how to get help in the VBA IDE:

Feature	Menu Command	Keyboard Shortcut
Request help from the Assistant*	Help⇨Microsoft Visual Basic Help	F1
Request help from the Assistant (Access)	Help⇨Microsoft Access Help	F1
Request help without bothering the Assistant	Help⇨Contents and Index	*none*

IntelliSense shortcuts

IntelliSense is way cool. Sort of like HAL-light (only fans of *2001: A Space Odyssey* will get that one). Here's the scoop on IntelliSense:

Feature	Menu Command	Keyboard Shortcut
List properties and methods for selected item	Edit⇨List Properties/Methods	Ctrl+J
List constants for selected item	Edit⇨List Constants	Ctrl+Shift+J

Feature	Menu Command	Keyboard Shortcut
List information for parameters	Edit⇨Parameter Info	Ctrl+Shift+I
Quick info (statement or function's definition) for selected item	Edit⇨Quick info	Ctrl+I
Complete the current word	Edit⇨Complete Word	Ctrl+Space

If you've checked the Auto List Members and Auto Quick Info checkboxes on the Editor tab (in Access, it's the Module tab) of the Options dialog box (Tools⇨Options), IntelliSense kicks in automatically when you create new statements. Then, these shortcuts are useful only when you need to edit an existing statement.

Other shortcuts

Here are some other miscellaneous, but useful things you can do in the VBA IDE:

Feature	Menu Command	Keyboard Shortcut
View or set various options	Tools⇨Options	*none*
View or set references	Tools⇨References	*none*
Manage toolbars	View⇨Toolbars	*none*

Running and debugging shortcuts

You use these shortcuts to debug and run your code:

Type	Feature	Menu Command	Keyboard Shortcut
Compiling	Compile project*	Debug⇨Compile Project	*none*
	Compile project (Access)	Debug⇨Compile All Modules	*none*
	Compile only currently loaded modules (Access only)	Debug⇨Compile Loaded Modules	*none*
	Compile and save entire project (Access only)	Debug⇨Compile and Save All Modules	*none*
Running	Run or continue running the current procedure*	Run⇨Run Sub/UserForm	F5

(continued)

Type	Feature	Menu Command	Keyboard Shortcut
	Run or continue running the current procedure (Access)	Run⇨Go/Continue	F5
Stopping	Temporarily halt running the current procedure*	Run⇨Break	Ctrl+Break
	Temporarily halt running the current procedure (Access)	*none*	Ctrl+Break
	Stop running current procedure and reset all variables	Run⇨Reset	*none*
	Stop running current procedure, but don't reset global variables (Access only)	Run⇨End	*none*
Stepping	Single step to the next line in the current procedure	Debug⇨Step Into	F8
	Single step to the next line in any procedure	Debug⇨Step Over	Shift+F8
	Continue running code in the current procedure and then start single stepping after exiting this procedure	Debug⇨Step Out	Ctrl+F8
	Designate the selected line of code as the next execution statement	Debug⇨ Set Next Statement	Ctrl+F9
	Move the cursor to the next executable statement (but don't actually execute it)	Debug⇨Show Next Statement	*none*

Search and replace operation shortcuts

VBA's global search and replace features can come in real handy. Here's a summary of the find and replace shortcuts:

Feature	Menu Command	Keyboard Shortcut
Find a text string	Edit⇨Find	Ctrl+F
Find the next instance of a text string	Edit⇨Find Next	F3
Replace one text string with another	Edit⇨Replace	Ctrl+H

Watch expressions

If you want to manage watch expressions, you need to master these shortcuts (hey, watch it):

Feature Shortcut	Menu Command	Keyboard
Create a watch expression	Debug⇨Add Watch	*none*
Create a watch for the selected expression	Debug⇨Quick Watch	Shift+F9
Edit an existing watch expression*	Debug⇨Edit Watch	Ctrl+W
Edit an existing watch expression (Access)	Debug⇨Edit Watch	*none*

Window management

If you have either too many or not enough windows displayed, check out these shortcuts:

Type	Feature	Menu Command	Keyboard Shortcut
Viewing	View the code associated with an object**	View⇨Code	F7
	View the object associated with a module**	View⇨Object	Shift+F7
Jumping	Jump to the definition of a selected item (if it's a built-in item, jump to its definition using the object browser)	View⇨Definition	Shift+F2
	Jump back to the previous selected item	View⇨Last Position	Ctrl+Shift+F2
Browsing	Open the object browser	View⇨Object Browser	F2
Opening	Open or shift focus to the Immediate window*	View⇨Immediate Window	Ctrl+G
	Open or shift focus to Debug window (Access)	View⇨Debug Window	Ctrl+G
	Open or shift focus to Locals Window**	View⇨Locals Window	*none*
	Open or shift focus to Watch window**	View⇨Watch Window	*none*
	Open Call Stack window	View⇨Call Stack	Ctrl+L

(continued)

Type	Feature	Menu Command	Keyboard Shortcut
	Open or shift focus to Project Explorer**	View⇨ Project Explorer	Ctrl+R
	Open or shift focus to Properties window**	View⇨ Properties Window	F4
	Open or close the toolbox**	View⇨Toolbox	*none*
	Open the Tab Order window**	View⇨Tab Order	*none*
Splitting	Split or unsplit the Code window	Window⇨Split	*none*
Arranging	Tile all open windows horizontally	Window⇨ Tile Horizontally	*none*
	Tile all open windows vertically	Window⇨ Tile Vertically	*none*
	Overlay all open windows	Window⇨Cascade	*none*
	Neatly arrange any minimized windows	Window⇨ Arrange Icons	*none*

Part II

Application Integration

One of the really cool things about VBA is that you can use it to execute and control other applications. This allows you to create integrated applications that are all tied together using Automation and VBA. The application integration features in VBA are sort of like the programming equivalent of the television remote control. So, for example, you can create and print form letters from a list of clients stored in your database, or perhaps you can use a charting program to print a chart of your client's sales.

In this part . . .

✔ **Creating integrated applications using Automation**

✔ **Starting other applications**

✔ **Activating an executing application**

✔ **Opening a file in another application**

Keyword Summary

Task	Keyword	Keyword Type
Activate an executing application	AppActivate	Statement
Create a reference to an Automation object	CreateObject	Function
Create a reference to an Automation object using a file	GetObject	Function
Start an application	Shell	Function

AppActivate (Statement)

Description: Activates an executing application.

Syntax:

```
AppActivate title [, wait]
```

Argument	Description
title	Title (in title bar) of running application. May be a partial match of title, or the task ID returned by the Shell function.
wait	Optional. Indicates whether VBA should wait until calling application has the focus before executing the AppActivate statement. Default is False.

Example: The following shifts the focus to any application whose title bar begins with "Microsoft Word":

```
AppActivate "Microsoft Word"
```

CreateObject (Function)

Description: Creates an Automation object and returns an object variable that points to it.

Syntax:

```
Set ojectvariable = CreateObject ( class )
```

Argument	Description
objectvariable	An object variable. Can be generic (As Object) or specific (As Excel.Application).
class	A string representing the class of an Automation object. The class argument must use the appname.objecttype syntax. Its parts are described here:

Argument	Description
appname —	The name of an Automation server application.
objecttype —	The type or class of Automation object to create.

Example: This example creates an Automation object that points to Excel's Application object. Because objExcell is typed using a generic object variable, the object is late bound:

```
Dim objExcell As Object
Set objExcell = CreateObject("Excel.Application")
```

This example also creates an Automation object that points to Excel's Application object. This time, however, objExcel2 is early bound because it is typed using a specific object variable (Excel.Application. Early bound means it's faster:

```
Dim objExcel2 As Excel.Application
Set objExcel2 = CreateObject("Excel.Application")
```

Notes: You use CreateObject when there is no existing instance of the object, or when you wish to create another instance of the object. If you wish to create a reference to an existing instance of an object or create an object using an existing file, use the GetObject function instead. If an object is registered as a single-instance object, however, CreateObject creates only one instance no matter how many times it executes.

Because the first example uses the generic object datatype, it employs late binding and is slower than the second example, which uses a specific object variable. (Note also that with late binding, many of the cool Intellisense features described in Part I are not available!) The second example, which employs early binding, however, requires you to first set a project reference to the Excel type library (or, more specifically, the Microsoft Excel 8.0 Object Library) using the Tools⇨References command.

You can also use the Set statement with the New keyword to create an object reference to an object. ***See also*** Set statement definition in Part XIV.

GetObject (Function)

Description: Creates an Automation object using a file or an existing instance of the application and returns an object variable that points to it.

Syntax:

```
Set objectvariable = GetObject ( [pathname,]
    [class] )
```

Argument	Description
`objectvariable`	An object variable. Can be generic (`As Object`) or specific (`As Excel.Application`).
`pathname`	Optional. Path and filename to a document of a registered Automation server application. Required if class is omitted.
`class`	Optional. A string representing the class of an Automation object. Required if pathname is omitted. The class argument must use the appname.objecttype syntax. Its parts are described here:
	`appname` — The name of an Automation server application.
	`objecttype` — The type or class of Automation object to create.

Example: This example creates an Automation object that points to an existing instance of Excel:

```
Dim objExcel1 As Object
Set objExcel1 = GetObject(,"Excel.Application")
```

This example creates an Automation object that loads the `calculator.xls` Excel workbook:

```
Dim objExcel2 As Object
Set objExcel2 = GetObject("c:\calculator.xls")
```

Notes: If you use the first form of `GetObject`, specifying only the classname of the object, an existing instance of the object must be running or a run-time error occurs. In this case, you may wish to use `CreateObject` instead.

If you use the second form of `GetObject`, specifying only the pathname argument, and an existing instance of the object is running, the document loads using the existing instance. If no existing instance is running, however, a new instance starts.

Because these examples use the generic object datatype, they employ late binding. *See also* the `CreateObject` statement definition in this Part for more details on early versus late binding.

Shell (Function)

Description: Starts an executable application and returns a `Double` containing its task ID if successful or zero if unsuccessful.

Syntax:

```
Shell ( pathname [, windowstyle] )
```

Argument	Description
pathname	Name of the executable program. If the program is not registered, you may need to include the path to the program.
windowstyle	Optional. A constant that designates the style of window for the application. May be one of the constants described in the following table.

Constant	Value	Description
vbHide	0	Window is hidden and receives the focus.
vbNormalFocus	1	Window is normal size and position and receives the focus.
vbMinimizedFocus	2	Window is minimized and receives the focus. The default.
vbMaximizedFocus	3	Window is maximized and receives the focus.
vbNormalNoFocus	4	Window is normal size and position but does not receive the focus.
vbMinimizedNoFocus	6	Window is minimized but does not receive the focus.

Example: This starts Notepad at normal size with focus. The dblTask variable contains the task ID of the new program:

```
dblTask = Shell("notepad", vbNormalFocus)
```

Part III

Arrays and Collections

Arrays have been a part of VBA and other BASIC dialects for ages. They are a great way to store lots of similar variables and treat them at times as if they were a single entity. You may use an array, for example, to store multiple records that you've read in from a file before processing the records. Then, using a loop (see Part VIII), you can process each of the records with very little code. VBA arrays can be multidimensional—that is, you can use a single array to store a customer's first name, last name, address, and so on.

Collections are a newer addition to the language. In some ways, they're not as flexible as arrays. For instance, collections can't be multidimensional. On the other hand, they're a lot easier to use when you just need to dump items into a list and retrieve them later because VBA handles most of the details of managing the collection for you. You may use a collection, for example, to store the names of several Visio shapes that you want to format similarly using VBA code.

In this part . . .

- ✔ Creating fixed-size and dynamic arrays
- ✔ Learning the syntax of VBA's keywords for creating and managing arrays
- ✔ Creating collections
- ✔ Learning the syntax of VBA's keywords for creating and managing collections

Keyword Summary

Task	Keyword	Keyword Type
Add an item to a collection	Add	Method
Change the default lower bound of arrays	Option Base	Statement
Count the number of items in a collection	Count	Property
Create a collection object	Collection	Keyword
Create an array from a list	Array	Function
Declare an array	Dim	Statement
Erase the contents of an array	Erase	Statement
Find the lower bound of an array	LBound	Function
Find the upper bound of an array	UBound	Function
Redimension a dynamic array	ReDim	Statement
Refer to an item in a collection	Item	Method
Remove an item from a collection	Remove	Method

Add (Method)

Description: Adds an item to a collection.

Syntax:

```
collection.Add item [, key] [, before] [, after]
```

Argument	Description
collection	A collection object.
item	The item you wish to add to the collection. May be the name of a variable or a string surrounded by quotes.
key	Optional. A string that uniquely identifies the item and that may be used to retrieve the item later. Defaults to no key.
before	Optional. An expression that identifies an existing item. The new item gets inserted into the collection *before* the existing item. If before is a number, then it refers to the item by position, where 1 is the position of the first item in a collection. If before is a string, then it refers to the item by key. If the before item doesn't exist, an error occurs. Defaults to none.

Argument	Description
after	Optional. An expression that identifies an existing item. The new item gets inserted into the collection *after* the existing item. If after is a number, then it refers to the item by position, where 1 is the position of the first item in a collection. If after is a string, then it refers to the item by key. If the after item doesn't exist, an error occurs. Defaults to none.

Example: The following items are inserted at end of the colFruit collection:

```
Dim colFruit As New Collection
colFruit.Add "apple"
colFruit.Add "orange"
```

Array (Function)

Description: Returns a Variant containing an array created from a list of items.

Syntax:

```
Array ( [list_of_items] )
```

Argument	Description
list_of_items	Optional. A list of numbers, strings, or variables separated by commas. If no items are specified, an empty array is created.

Example: Create an array of variants with four elements:

```
Dim varArray As Variant
varArray = Array(1, 2, 3, "pie")
```

Notes: Array places the array inside of a scalar Variant variable, which is not the same as an array of Variants. In fact, the Variant assigned to the array *cannot* be defined as an array.

The first element of the array has an index of 0, unless you've used Option Base. (*Note:* VBA online help says that arrays created with the Array function always have an index of 0 regardless of the Option Base setting, but this is wrong.)

Collection (Keyword)

Description: Creates a collection object when used in a `Dim` or `Set` statement.

Syntax: You can use the `Collection` keyword along with the `New` keyword and either the `Dim` or `Set` statement to create a collection. The first way, using only a single `Dim` statement, looks like this:

```
Dim collection As New Collection
```

The second way to do this, which uses a `Dim` keyword (without `New`) and a `Set` statement with the `New` keyword looks like this:

```
Dim collection As Collection
Set collection = New Collection
```

Argument	Description
collection	Name of collection.

Example: Creates a new collection named `colFruit`:

```
Dim colFruit As New Collection
```

Notes: The two ways to create a collection are equivalent.

Count (Property)

Description: Returns a `Long` containing the number of items in a collection. A read-only property.

Syntax:

```
collection.Count
```

Argument	Description
collection	Name of a collection.

Example:

```
Dim colFruit As New Collection
colFruit.Add "apple"
colFruit.Add "banana"
lngItems = colFruit.Count '= 2
```

Dim (Statement)

Description: In addition to its other users, the Dim statement can be used to create an array.

Syntax: Two forms of the Dim statement create arrays:

```
Dim arrayvariable( [lowerbound To] upperbound
    [, ...] ) [As datatype]
Dim arrayvariable() [As datatype]
```

As you can see, two versions of the Dim statement exist. (Actually, there are more versions for non-array variables, but that's a whole other story that appears in Part XIV.) The first version creates a fixed-size array (sometimes also know as a *static array*); the second creates a *dynamic array.*

Argument	Description
arrayvariable	Name of array variable.
upperbound	Required for fixed-size arrays. Specifies the upper bound of the array.
lowerbound	Optional for fixed-size arrays. Specifies the lower bound of the array. Defaults to 0 unless you've used the Option Base statement.
datatype	Optional. The datatype that each element of the array will be assigned. Defaults to Variant.

Example: This example creates a dynamic array of integers:

```
Dim intAges() As Integer
```

This example creates a fixed-size array of 101 strings (unless you've used the Option Base 1 statement, which would give you an array of 100 strings):

```
Dim strNames(100) As String
```

This creates a fixed-size 2-dimensional array of 1000 (10 x 100) strings:

```
Dim strNames(1 To 100, 1 To 10) As String
```

Notes: Before you can use a dynamic array, you must use the ReDim statement.

Erase (Statement)

Description: Reinitializes the array.

Syntax:

```
Erase arraylist
```

Argument	Description
arraylist	One or more array variables.

Example:

```
Erase datBirthDates
Erase strFruits, varMeats
```

Notes: When used with a fixed-size array, Erase reinitializes the elements. When used with a dynamic array, Erase also resets the array to its initialized state, releasing any dynamic memory consumed by the array.

Item (Method)

Description: Returns an item in a collection.

Syntax:

```
collection.Item(index)
```

Argument	Description
collection	A collection object.
index	An index to the item you wish to retrieve from the collection. If the index is a number, VBA retrieves the item by its position in the collection. If the index is a string, VBA retrieves the item by its key value.

Example: Create the colFruit collection with three items:

```
Dim colFruit As New Collection
colFruit.Add "apple" , "a"
colFruit.Add "orange", "o"
colFruit.Add "peach", "p"
```

Use the item method to grab the third item (peach):

```
varFifth = colFruit.Item(3)    '= peach
```

Because Item is the default method of a collection, you can also retrieve the third item using:

```
varFifth = colFruit(3)          '= peach
```

The following example uses the key to retrieve the second item (orange):

```
varApple = colFruit.Item("o") '= orange
```

LBound (Function)

Description: Returns a Long containing the lower bound of an array.

Syntax:

```
LBound ( arrayname [, dimension] )
```

Argument	Description
arrayname	Name of array.
dimension	Optional. The dimension of the array to check. Defaults to first dimension.

Example: Declare a two-dimensional fixed-size array:

```
Dim dblFuel(0 To 100, 1 To 35) As Double
```

Find the lower-bound of the first dimension:

```
lngLower1 = LBound(dblFuel, 1) '= 0
```

Because the first dimension is the default, this also produces the same result:

```
lngLower2 = LBound(dblFuel)      '= 0
```

Notes: Using LBound with an initialized dynamic array (before a ReDim statement) causes a runtime error.

Option Base (Statement)

Description: Sets the default lower bound for arrays in a module.

Syntax:

```
Option Base number
```

Argument	Description
number	The default lower bound for arrays. May be 0 or 1.

Example: Set the default lower bound of arrays to 1:

```
Option Base 1
```

Notes: Must appear in the *declarations* section of a module. If the module contains no `Option Base` statement, the default lower bound for arrays is `0`.

ReDim (Statement)

Description: Sizes or resizes a dynamic array.

Syntax:

```
ReDim [Preserve] arrayvariable( [lowerbound To]
    upperbound [, ...] ) [As datatype]
```

Argument	Description
Preserve	Optional. When included, the array's existing elements are preserved as the array is resized. When Preserve is omitted, VBA performs destructive resizing (all elements are reinitialized).
arrayvariable	Name of array variable.
upperbound	Specifies the upper bound of the array.
lowerbound	Optional. Specifies the lower bound of the array. Defaults to 0 unless you've used the Option Base statement.
datatype	Optional. Specifies the datatype of elements for arrays contained in a Variant; otherwise this argument does not apply.

Example: Define a dynamic array of longs:

```
Dim lngCounts() As Long
```

Use `ReDim` to size the array:

```
ReDim lngCounts(1 To 5, 1 To 20)
```

Use `ReDim` to resize the array while preserving the existing elements :

```
ReDim Preserve lngCounts(1 to 5, 1 To 25)
```

Notes: If using the `Preserve` keyword with arrays of two or more dimensions, you can't change the upperbound of any dimension except the last. In addition, when using `Preserve`, you can't change the lowerbound of *any* dimensions.

You can use "As datatype" only for destructively resized arrays contained in a Variant (may not be used with the Preserve keyword).

Remove (Method)

Description: Removes an item from a collection.

Syntax:

collection.**Remove** index

Argument	Description
collection	A collection object.
index	An index to the item you wish to remove from the collection. If the index is a number, VBA identifies the item by its position in the collection. If the index is a string, VBA identifies the item by its key value.

Example: The following removes the twelfth item from the collection:

colFruit.Remove 12

The following removes the item with a key value of "b":

colFruit.Remove "b"

UBound (Function)

Description: Returns a Long containing the upper bound of an array.

Syntax:

UBound (arrayname [,dimension])

Argument	Description
arrayname	Name of array.
dimension	Optional. The dimension of the array to check. Defaults to first dimension.

Example: Declare a two-dimensional fixed-size array:

Dim dblFuel(0 To 100, 1 To 35) As Double

Find the upper-bound of the first dimension:

```
lngUpper1 = UBound(dblFuel, 1) '= 100
```

Because the first dimension is the default, this also produces the same result:

```
lngUpper2 = UBound(dblFuel)      '= 100
```

Notes: Using `UBound` with an initialized dynamic array (before a `ReDim` statement) causes a runtime error.

Part IV

Conversion

VBA is pretty smart about converting values. For example, if you place an `Integer` value into a `Double` variable, VBA automatically handles the conversion for you. Sometimes, however, you'd like more control over the conversion process — after all, you are the programmer. That's where the conversion functions come in handy.

If you don't find the function you're looking for here, you may want to check out Parts V or XII, which contain some related functions.

In this part . . .

✔ **Using the VBA conversion functions**

✔ **Learning how to force the conversion to a specific datatype**

✔ **Learning how to format strings using the versatile** `Format` **function**

✔ **Converting decimal numbers into hexadecimal and octal numbers**

Keyword Summary

Task	Keyword	Keyword Type
Change a decimal value to hexadecimal	Hex	Function
Change a decimal value to octal	Oct	Function
Convert a character into a character code	Asc	Function
Convert a character code into a character	Chr	Function
Convert an expression into a Boolean value	CBool	Function
Convert an expression into a Byte value	CByte	Function
Convert an expression into a Currency value	CCur	Function
Convert an expression into a Date value	CDate	Function
Convert an expression into a Double value	CDbl	Function
Convert an expression into a Decimal value	CDec	Function
Convert an expression into an Integer value	CInt	Function
Convert an expression into an Long value	CLng	Function
Convert an expression into an Single value	CSng	Function
Convert an expression into an Variant value	CVar	Function
Convert an expression into an String value	CStr	Function
Convert a number to a string	Str	Function
Convert a string to a number	Val	Function
Format a value as a string using a template	Format	Function
Truncate a number	Fix, Int	Function

Asc (Function)

Description: Converts a character into an Integer containing the equivalent character code.

Syntax:

Asc (*string*)

Argument	Description
string	A string.

Example:

```
intCode = Asc("b")   '= 98
```

Notes: All characters other than the first are ignored. When used with a Null or zero-length string, Asc causes an error.

CBool (Function)

Description: Converts an expression into a Boolean (True/False) value.

Syntax:

CBool (*expression*)

Argument	Description
expression	A numeric or Boolean expression.

Example:

```
fConv1 = CBool(34)        '= True
fConv2 = Cbool(100 > 10)  '= True
fConv3 = Cbool(100 < 10)  '= False
fConv4 = CBool(0)         '= False
```

Notes: All non-zero numbers, return True; zero returns False.

CByte (Function)

Description: Converts an expression into a Byte value.

Syntax:

CByte (*expression*)

Argument	Description
expression	A number between 0 and 255; fractions are rounded.

Example:

```
bytConv = CByte(200.58)   '= 201
```

CCur (Function)

Description: Converts an expression into a Currency value.

Syntax:

CCur (*expression*)

Argument	Description
expression	A number between -922,337,203,685,477.5808 and 922,337,203,685,477.5807.

Example:

```
curConv = CCur(45678.908155)   '= 45678.9082
```

CDate (Function)

Description: Converts an expression into a Date value.

Syntax:

```
CDate ( expression )
```

Argument	Description
expression	A valid date expression.

Example: Convert the number of days from December 30, 1899 into a Date value:

```
datConv1 = CDate(25678.9) '= 4/20/70 9:36:00 PM
```

Convert a date expression into a date value:

```
datConv2 = CDate(#3/4/2#) '= 3/4/2002
```

Notes: CVDate works the same as CDate, but returns a Variant whose subtype is Date.

Dates with two-digit years less than 30 are assumed to be 21st century dates; otherwise, they are assumed to be 20th century dates. Because of the impending century change, it's best to use four-digit years as much as possible.

 When working with dates, it's a good idea to surround all literal date/time expressions with pound signs (#) which is the date/time delimiter. If you don't, VBA may not interpret the date correctly.

CDbl (Function)

Description: Converts an expression into a Double value.

Syntax:

```
CDbl ( expression )
```

Argument	Description
expression	A number equal to 0 or, if negative, between -1.80E308 and -4.94E-324; if positive, between 4.94E-324 and 1.80E308.

Example:

```
dblConv = CDbl("-4.5")   '= -4.5
```

CDec (Function)

Description: Converts an expression into a Decimal value.

Syntax:

```
CDec ( expression )
```

Argument	Description
expression	A number whose range varies depending on the number of decimal places. For a number with zero decimal places, it may range between -7.9E28 and 7.9E28. For a number with 28 decimal places, it may range between -7.9 and 7.9.

Example:

```
varConv = CDec(-7.9E5) '= -790000
```

Notes: Because there is no Decimal datatype, CDec returns a Variant whose subtype is Decimal.

Chr (Function)

Description: Converts a character code into a character String.

Syntax:

```
Chr ( charcode )
```

Argument	Description
charcode	A Long number normally ranging between 0 and 255. On double-byte character systems, it may range between -32,768 and 65,536.

Example:

```
strChar = Chr(65) '= "A"
```

CInt (Function)

Description: Converts an expression into a Integer value.

Syntax:

CInt (*expression*)

Argument	Description
expression	A number between -32,768 and 32,767; fractions are rounded.

Example:

intConv = CInt(5178.71)   '= 5179

Notes: Fractional numbers are rounded by CInt.

CLng (Function)

Description: Converts an expression into a Long value.

Syntax:

CLng (*expression*)

Argument	Description
expression	A number between -2,147,483,648 and 2,147,483,647; fractions are rounded.

Example:

lngConv = CLng(45678.437)   '= 45678

Notes: Fractional numbers are rounded by CLng.

CSng (Function)

Description: Converts an expression into a Single value.

Syntax:

CSng (*expression*)

Argument	Description
expression	A number equal to 0 or, if negative, between -3.40E38 and -1.40E-45; if positive, between 1.40E-45 and 3.40E38.

Example:
```
sngConv = CSng(45678.908155)   '= 45678.91
```

Notes: Numbers are rounded as they are converted by CSng.

CStr (Function)

Description: Converts an expression into a String value.

Syntax:
```
CStr ( expression )
```

Argument	Description
expression	A string with a length of between 0 and approximately 2 billion characters.

Example:
```
strConv1 = CStr(4 & "chickens") '= "4 chickens"
strConv2 = CStr(-3.458)         '= "-3.458"
```

CVar (Function)

Description: Converts an expression into a Variant value.

Syntax:
```
CVar ( expression )
```

Argument	Description
expression	For numbers, the same range as for CDbl. For strings, the same range as for CStr.

Example:
```
varConv1 = CVar(45678.908155)   '= "45678.908155"
varConv2 = CVar(4 & "chickens") '= "4 chickens"
```

Fix (Function)

Description: Truncates an expression into a whole number.

Syntax:
```
Fix ( number )
```

Argument	Description
number	A numeric expression not to exceed the limits of a Double number.

Example:

```
intFix1 = Fix(23+6/13)         '= 23
dblFix2 = Fix(-236343434.9) '= -236343434
```

Notes: The datatype returned by Fix is based on the size of the input expression and may be Integer, Long, or Double.

For negative numbers, Fix returns the first negative whole number greater than or equal to the expression. This differs from the behavior of Int, which returns the first negative whole number less than or equal to the expression. Other than this difference, the two functions are identical.

Fix (and Int) truncate the fractional portion of a number; if you wish to round the number, use CInt or CLng instead.

Format (Function)

Description: Formats a value as a Variant string using a template.

Syntax:

```
Format ( expression [, format] [, firstdayofweek]
    [, firstweekofyear] )
```

Argument	Description
expression	A valid expression.
format	Optional. A format template; either named or user-defined. Defaults to no template, which causes Format to simply convert the expression into a String. See lists of format templates following this list of arguments.
firstdayofweek	Optional. A constant that specifies the first day of the week (vbUseSystem, vbSunday, vbMonday, ..., vbSaturday). Defaults to your Windows control panel date setting.
firstweekofyear	Optional. A constant that specifies the first week of the year (vbUseSystem, vbFirstJan1, vbFirstFourDays, vbFirstFullWeek) Defaults to your Windows control panel date setting.

Numeric formats

Use one of these format templates to convert the expression using standard numeric formats:

Format	Description
General Number	Number without thousands separator.
Currency	Currency.
Fixed	Number with two digits to right of decimal point.
Standard	Same as Fixed, with the addition of thousands separator.
Percent	• Percent value.
Scientific	Using scientific notation.
Yes/No	No if 0; otherwise, display Yes. (You can also use True/False or On/Off.)

User-defined numeric formats

Use one or more of these user-defined format template characters to convert the expression into a custom number:

Character	Description
0	A digit or 0.
#	A digit or nothing.
.	Decimal placeholder
%	Percentage placeholder.
,	Thousand separator.
E	Scientific notation character.
-+$( )	Literal character.
\	Display the next character literally.
"xyz"	Display characters within quotes literally.

Named date/time formats

Use one of these format templates to convert the expression using standard date/time formats:

Format	Description
General Date	System short date with time.
Long Date	System long date.
Medium Date	Medium date appropriate for host language.

Format	Description
Short Date	System short date.
Long Time	System long time (includes hours, minutes, and seconds).
Medium Time	12-hour format with AM/PM.
Short Time	24-hour format.

User-defined date/time formats

Use one or more of these user-defined format template characters to convert the expression into a custom date:

Character	Description
:	Time separator.
/	Date separator.
c	System short date with time (4/5/58 4:05:03 AM).
d	Numeric day without leading zero (5).
dd	Numeric day with a leading zero (05).
ddd	Abbreviated string for day of week (Sat).
dddd	Full string for day of week (Saturday).
ddddd	Complete short date. (4/5/58).
dddddd	Complete long date (Saturday, April 5, 1958).
w	Numeric day of week (7).
ww	Numeric week of year (14).
m	Numeric month without leading zero (4).
mm	Numeric month with leading zero (04).
mmm	Abbreviated string for month (Apr).
mmmm	Full string for month (April).
q	Numeric quarter without leading zero (2).
y	Day of year with leading zero (95).
yy	Year as two-digit number with leading zero (58).
yyyy	Year as four-digit number (1958).
h	Hour without leading zero (4).
hh	Hour with leading zero (04).
n	Minute without leading zero (5).
nn	Minute with leading zero (05).
s	Second without leading zero (3).
ss	Minute with leading zero (03).

Character	Description
ttttt	Complete time (4:05:03 AM).
AM/PM	Display times with uppercase AM or PM indicator (am/pm is identical except it is displayed in lowercase).
A/P	Display times with uppercase A or P indicator (a/p is identical except it is displayed in lowercase).
AMPM	Display times with the system AM or PM indicator.

User-defined string formatting

Use one or more of these user-defined format template characters to convert the expression into a custom string:

Character	Description
@	Character or space.
&	Character or nothing.
<	Force all characters lowercase.
>	Force all characters uppercase.
!	Force left to right fill of placeholders. Default is right to left.

Example:

```
varFmt1 = Format(23, "Fixed")              '= "23.00"
varFmt2 = Format(23, "0,000.##")           '= "0,023."
varFmt3 = Format("hello", ">")             '= "HELLO"
varFmt4 = Format("4/5/1958","mmm-dd")      '= "Apr-05"
```

Notes: When using user-defined numeric formats, you may specify up to four sections separated with semicolons. If you supply all four sections, then the first is used for positive values, the second for negative values, the third for zero values, and the fourth for Null values. If you supply only one section, the format applies to all values. For example, the following Format function returns "23.5" if varNumber=23.5, "(23.5)" if varNumber=-23.5, "0" if varNumber=0, and "Null" if varNumber is Null:

```
varFmt7 = Format(varNumber, "#.#;(#.#);0;\N\u\l\l")
```

When using user-defined string formats, you may specify up to two sections separated with semicolons. If you supply both sections, then the first is used for normal values and the second section for Null values and zero-length strings. If you supply only one section, the format applies to all values. For example, the following Format function returns "RED" if varString="red", or "Unknown" if varString is Null or a zero-length string:

```
varFmt8 = Format(varString, ">;\U\n\k\n\o\w\n")
```

Hex (Function)

Description: Converts a decimal value into a `Variant` containing a hexadecimal value.

Syntax:

Hex (*number*)

Argument	Description
number	A numeric expression. If Null, returns `Null`; if Empty, returns 0; otherwise returns an hexadecimal number with up to eight digits.

Example:

varHex = Hex(709) '= 2C5

Int (Function)

Description: Truncates an expression into a whole number.

Syntax:

Int (*number*)

Argument	Description
number	A numeric expression not to exceed the limits of a `Double` number.

Example:

```
intInt1 = Int(23+6/13)        '= 23
dblInt2 = Int(-236343434.9)  '= -236343435
```

Notes: The datatype returned by `Int` is based on the size of the input expression and may be `Integer`, `Long`, or `Double`.

For negative numbers, `Int` returns the first negative whole number less than or equal to the input expression. This differs from the behavior of `Fix`, which returns the first negative whole number greater than or equal to the expression. Other than this difference, the two functions are identical.

Int (and `Fix`) truncate the fractional portion of a number; if you wish to round the number, use `CInt` or `CLng` instead.

Oct (Function)

Description: Converts a decimal value into a `Variant` containing a octal value.

Syntax:

`Oct ( number )`

Argument	Description
number	A numeric expression. If Null, returns `Null`; if Empty, returns 0; otherwise returns an octal number with up to 11 digits.

Example:

`varOct = Oct(709) '= 1305`

Str (Function)

Description: Converts a number into a `Variant` string.

Syntax:

`Str( number )`

Argument	Description
number	A numeric expression.

Example:

`varStr = Str(139.893) '= "139.893"`

Val (Function)

Description: Converts a string into a `Double` number.

Syntax:

`Val ( string )`

Argument	Description
string	A string.

Example:

```
varVal1 = Val("tunafish")   '= 0
varVal2 = Val("14tunas")    '= 14
varVal3 = Val("234.9")      '= 234.9
```

Part V

Date and Time Manipulation

VBA includes numerous functions for manipulating dates and times. This rich set of functions makes calculating the difference between two dates, extracting any part of a date, timing a process, or creating a date or time value from its constituent parts easy. Mind you, it wasn't always this easy. Earlier versions of BASIC and other languages required you to do all this stuff yourself. So have fun with your date and time keywords, and learn to appreciate how easy you have it!

In this part . . .

✔ **Calculating the difference between two dates**

✔ **Extracting a portion of a date or time value**

✔ **Determining the system date and/or time**

✔ **Setting the system date or time**

✔ **Timing a process**

Keyword Summary

Task	Keyword	KeywordType
Add or subtract two dates	`DateAdd`	Function
Create a date from a string	`DateValue`	Function
Create a date from numeric parts	`DateSerial`	Function
Create a time from a string	`TimeValue`	Function
Create a time from numeric parts	`TimeSerial`	Function
Extract a specific portion of a date	`DatePart`	Function
Extract the day portion of a date	`Day`	Function
Extract the hours portion of a time	`Hour`	Function
Extract the minutes portion of a time	`Minute`	Function
Extract the month portion of a date	`Month`	Function
Extract the seconds portion of a time	`Second`	Function
Extract the weekday portion of a date	`Weekday`	Function
Extract the year portion of a date	`Year`	Function
Find the difference between two dates	`DateDiff`	Function
Retrieve the current time	`Time`	Function
Retrieve the current date	`Date`	Function
Retrieve the current date with time	`Now`	Function
Set the system date	`Date`	Statement
Set the system time	`Time`	Statement
Time a process	`Timer`	Function

Date (Function)

Description: Returns the current system date.

Syntax:

```
Date()
```

Example: Assuming today's date is 6/19/1998:

```
varToday = Date()  '= 6/19/98
```

Date (Statement)

Description: Sets the current system date.

Syntax:

```
Date = date
```

Argument	Description
date	A valid date string; for Windows 95 must be between 1/1/1980 and 12/31/2099; for Windows NT must be between 1/1/1980 and 12/31/2079; for Macintosh must be between 1/1/1904 and 2/5/2040.

Example:

```
Date = #4/26/1998# 'Sets system date to 4/26/1998
```

Notes: When working with dates and times, it's a good idea to surround all literal date/time expressions with pound signs (#), which is the date/time delimiter. If you don't, VBA may not interpret the date/time correctly. In addition, because of the impending century change, it's best to use four-digit years as much as possible.

DateAdd (Function)

Description: Adds or subtracts two date/time values.

Syntax:

```
DateAdd ( interval, number, date )
```

Argument	Description
interval	String expression representing interval of date/time you wish to add or subtract. See Interval argument settings below.
number	If positive, number of intervals to add to date; if negative, number of intervals to subtract from date.
date	A date/time expression.

Interval argument settings:

Setting	Description	Setting	Description
yyyy	Year	w	Weekday
q	Quarter	ww	Week
m	Month	h	Hour
y	Day of year	n	Minute
d	Day	s	Second

Example: In the following example, varAdd equals 4/26/97

```
varAdd = DateAdd("yyyy",39,#4/26/58#)
```

In the following example, varAdd equals 1/1/98 2:30:00 PM

```
varDif = DateAdd("h",-4, #1/1/98 18:30#)
```

DateDiff (Function)

Description: Returns the difference between two date/time expressions.

Syntax:

```
DateDiff ( interval, date1, date2
     [, firstdayofweek] [, firstweekofyear] )
```

Argument	Description
interval	String expression representing interval of date/time you wish to add or subtract. (**See also** DateAdd function for a list of possible interval arguments).
date1	A date/time expression.
date2	A date/time expression.
firstdayofweek	Optional. A constant that specifies the first day of the week (vbUseSystem, vbSunday, vbMonday, ..., vbSaturday). Defaults to your Windows control panel date setting.
firstweekofyear	Optional. A constant that specifies the first week of the year (vbUseSystem, vbFirstJan1, vbFirstFourDays, vbFirstFullWeek) Defaults to your Windows control panel date setting.

Example:

```
varDif = DateDiff("m",#1/31/98#, #2/1/98#) '= 1
```

Notes: DateDiff returns the number of discrete interval units between two dates. Thus the difference in months between 1/31/98 and 2/1/98 is 1; the difference in months between 1/1/98 and 1/31/98 is 0.

If date2 occurs prior to date1, DateDiff returns a negative value.

DatePart (Function)

Description: Returns a specified portion of date/time expression as a number.

```
DatePart ( interval, date [, firstdayofweek]
    [, firstweekofyear] )
```

Argument	Description
interval	String expression representing interval of date/time you wish to extract. (**See also** DateAdd function for a list of possible interval arguments).
date	A date/time expression.
firstdayofweek	Optional. A constant that specifies the first day of the week (vbUseSystem, vbSunday, vbMonday, ..., vbSaturday). Defaults to your Windows control panel date setting.
firstweekofyear	Optional. A constant that specifies the first week of the year (vbUseSystem, vbFirstJan1, vbFirstFourDays, vbFirstFullWeek) Defaults to your Windows control panel date setting.

Example:

```
varPart = DatePart("q", #7/13/99#)  '= 3
```

DateSerial (Function)

Description: Returns a date value from its numeric parts.

Syntax:

```
DateSerial ( year, month, day )
```

Argument	Description
year	An integer representing the year portion of a date. If value is between 0 and 99, it is assumed to be a two-digit year. Two-digit years less than 30 are assumed to be 21st Century dates; otherwise, they are assumed to be 20th Century dates.
month	An integer representing the month portion of a date.
day	An integer representing the day portion of a date.

Example:

```
varDate1 = DateSerial(1776, 7, 4)   '= 7/4/1776
```

Notes: When any argument is outside the normal range of values for a date, VBA increments or decrements the next larger unit as appropriate. Thus, in the following example, VBA takes 1/1/1997 and subtracts 6 months and 15 days, returning 5/16/1996:

```
varDate2 = DateSerial(1997,-6,-15) '= 5/16/96
```

DateValue (Function)

Description: Returns a date value from a string.

Syntax:

```
DateValue  )
```

Argument	Description
date	A string expression representing a date/time between 1/1/0100 and 12/31/9999.

Example:

```
varDate = DateValue("3/13/2001 13:43") '= 3/13/2001
```

Notes: Any time portion of a date/time value is truncated.

Day (Function)

Description: Returns an Integer (between 1 and 31) representing the day portion of a date/time value.

Syntax:

```
Day ( date )
```

Argument	Description
date	A date/time expression between 1/1/0100 and 12/31/9999.

Example:

```
varDay = Day(#3/4/1976 04:23:16 pm#) '= 4
```

Hour (Function)

Description: Returns an Integer (between 0 and 23) representing the hour portion of a date/time value.

Syntax:

```
Hour ( time )
```

Argument	Description
time	A date/time expression between 1/1/0100 and 12/31/9999.

Example:
```
varHour = Hour(#3/4/1976 04:23:16 pm#)'= 4
```

Minute (Function)

Description: Returns an Integer (between 0 and 59) representing the minute portion of a date/time value.

Syntax:

Minute (*time*)

Argument	Description
time	A date/time expression between 1/1/0100 and 12/31/9999.

Example:
```
varHour = Minute(#3/4/1976 04:23:16 pm#)'= 23
```

Month (Function)

Description: Returns an Integer (between 1 and 12) representing the month portion of a date/time value.

Syntax:

Month (*date*)

Argument	Description
date	A date/time expression between 1/1/0100 and 12/31/9999.

Example:
```
varMonth = Month(#3/4/1976 04:23:16 pm#) '= 3
```

Now (Function)

Description: Returns the current system date and time.

Syntax:

Now()

Example: Assuming today's date is 6/19/1998 and the time is 4:01:36 PM:

```
varNow = Now() '= 6/19/98 4:01:36 PM
```

Second (Function)

Description: Returns an Integer (between 0 and 59) representing the second portion of a date/time value.

Syntax:

Second (*time*)

Argument	Description
time	A date/time expression between 1/1/0100 and 12/31/9999.

Example:
varSecond = Second(#3/4/1976 04:23:16 pm#) '= 16

Time (Function)

Description: Returns the current system time.

Syntax:

Time()

Example: Assuming the time is 4:01:36 PM:

varTime = Time() '= 4:01:36 PM

Time (Statement)

Description: Sets the current system time.

Syntax:

Time = *time*

Argument	Description
date	A valid time string.

Example:

Time = #13:00# 'Sets system time to 1:00:00 PM

Timer (Function)

Description: Returns a Single representing the number of seconds (and fractional seconds) since midnight.

Syntax:

Timer()

Example: The following example shows how you might use the
Timer function to time a process:

```
Dim sngStart As Single
Dim sngDuration As Single
sngStart = Timer()
' ...additional code running some process...
sngDuration = Timer() - sngStart
```

TimeSerial (Function)

Description: Returns a time value from its numeric parts.

Syntax:

TimeSerial (*hour, minute, second*)

Argument	Description
hour	An Integer (between 0 and 23) representing the hours portion of a time.
minute	An Integer representing the minutes portion of a time.
second	An Integer representing the seconds portion of a time.

Example:

```
varTime1 = TimeSerial(23,14,45) '= 11:14:45 PM
```

Notes: When any argument is outside the normal range of values
for a time, VBA increments or decrements the next larger unit as
appropriate. Thus, in the following example, VBA takes 1:16 AM
and subtracts 5 minutes, returning 12:55:16 AM:

```
varTime2 = TimeSerial(1,-5,16) '= 12:55:16 AM
```

TimeValue (Function)

Description: Returns a time value from a string.

Syntax:

TimeValue (*time*)

Parameters:

Argument	Description
time	A string expression representing a date/time between 1/1/0100 and 12/31/9999. If time equals only the time portion of a date/time, it must be between 00:00:00 and 23:59:59.

Example:
```
varTime1 = TimeValue("3/13/98 13:43")  '= 1:43:00 PM
varTime2 = TimeValue("13:43")          '= 1:43:00 PM
```

Notes: Any date portion of a date/time value is truncated.

Weekday (Function)

Description: Returns an Integer (between 1 and 7) representing the weekday portion of a date/time value.

Syntax:
```
Weekday ( date [, firstdayofweek] )
```

Parameters:

Argument	Description
date	A date/time expression between 1/1/0100 and 12/31/9999.
firstdayofweek	Optional. A constant that specifies the first day of the week (vbUseSystem, vbSunday, vbMonday, ..., vbSaturday). Defaults to your Windows control panel date setting.

Example:
```
varWD = Weekday(#3/4/76 04:23:16 #, vbMonday) '= 4
```

Year (Function)

Description: Returns an Integer (between 100 and 9999) representing the year portion of a date/time value.

Syntax:
```
Year ( date )
```

Parameters:

Argument	Description
date	A date/time expression between 1/1/0100 and 12/31/9999.

Example:
```
varYear = Year(#3/4/1976 04:23:16 pm#) '= 1976
```

Part VI

Debugging and Error Handling

In a perfect world, errors don't occur. But we all know that the world ain't perfect. One way to handle errors in your code is to ignore them and let VBA deal with them — but then again, we usually like to get paid for our work. VBA comes with a host of error-handling keywords and the Err object to trap and handle runtime errors.

VBA also supports the use of the Debug object, which makes it quite easy to write debugging messages to the Immediate window.

In this part . . .

- ✔ **Writing debugging information to the Immediate window**
- ✔ **Trapping runtime errors**
- ✔ **Determining which error has occurred**
- ✔ **Handling runtime errors**
- ✔ **Generating user-defined errors**
- ✔ **Returning error codes to calling procedures**

Keyword Summary

Task	Keyword	Keyword Type
Determine the message associated with an error	Error	Function
Generate a runtime error	Raise	Method
Manage runtime errors	Err	Object
Print text to the Immediate window	Debug	Object
Reset the Err object	Clear	Method
Resume program execution after a runtime error	Resume	Statement
Return a user-defined error	CVErr	Function
Trap errors at runtime	On Error	Statement

Clear (Method)

Description: A method of the Err object used to reset the error state.

Syntax:

```
Err.Clear
```

Argument	Description
Err	The error object.

Example:

```
Err.Clear
```

Notes: Clear is automatically called when VBA encounters any Resume, Exit Sub, Exit Function, Exit Property, or On Error statement.

CVErr (Function)

Description: Returns a Variant of subtype Error. Useful for creating user-defined errors.

Syntax:

```
CVErr ( errornumber )
```

Parameter	*Description*
errornumber	A Long between 0 and 65,535.

Example: The following function, DivideIt, returns an user-defined error when lngDenom = 0:

```
Function DivideIt(lngNum, lngDenom) As Variant
    If lngDenom <> 0 Then
        DivideIt = CDbl(lngNum) / CDbl(lngDenom)
    Else
        DivideIt = CVErr(10001)
    End If
End Function
```

These examples test out DivideIt, first with a non-zero lngDenom argument and then with a zero lngDenom argument:

```
varDividend1 = DivideIt(5,7)  '= 0.714285714285714
varDividend2 = DivideIt(5,0)  '= Error 10001
```

Notes: You can use the IsError function (***see also*** Part XIV) to test if a return value from a function is an Error subtype.

Built-in error codes are generally in the range of 0 to 4000, so creating user-defined error codes outside this range is best.

Debug (Object)

Description: Used to print text to the Immediate window.

Syntax:

Debug.*method*

The Debug object has no properties and one method, Print.

Example:

```
Debug.Print "Hi there!"
```

Notes: You can use the debug object to log information to the Immediate window, which is useful when debugging programs.

Err (Object)

Description: Contains information about runtime errors.

Syntax:

Err.*method_or_property*

The Err object has several properties and methods:

Type	Property/Method	Description
Method	Clear	Explicitly resets Err to a non-error state.
Method	Raise	Generates a runtime error.
Property	Description	The message associated with an error. Read/write.
Property	HelpContext	A help file context ID for the error. Read/write.
Property	HelpFile	A help file for the error. Read/write.
Property	LastDLLError	Contains the system error code for the last call to an external DLL. (32-bit Windows platforms only). Read only.
Property	Number	The error code for the error. Read/write. Number is the default property of the Err object.
Property	Source	Name of the VBA project or application that generated the error. Read/write.

Example: This example places the error number for last VBA error into lngErrNum:

```
lngErrNum = Err.Number
```

This example places the error message for last VBA error into strErrMsg:

```
strErrMsg = Err.Description
```

Notes: See also the Clear and Raise method definitions in this part for more details on their syntax.

Error (Function)

Description: Returns a String containing the error message associated with an error number.

Syntax:

```
Error ( [errornumber] )
```

Argument	Description
errornumber	Optional. A Long between 0 and 65,535. If errornumber is within this range, but there is no associated error, Error returns "Application-defined or object-defined error". Defaults to the message associated with the most recent runtime error.

Example:

```
strErrMsg = Error(6) ' = "Overflow"
```

Notes:

When used without an errornumber argument, Error is equivalent to using the Description property of the Err object.

On Error (Statement)

Description: Enables an error trap or in-line error handling. Can also be used to disable error handling.

Syntax:

There are three forms of the On Error statement:

Statement Form	Description
On Error GoTo line	Enables an *error trap*. Line is a line number or label that points to a statement in the current procedure where execution should jump to when a runtime error occurs. When an error occurs, VBA will not notify the user of the error, but will otherwise act as if an error occurred, filling the Err object with information about the error. Code within the error trap can use the Err object to determine which error has occurred and what to do about it.
On Error Resume Next	Enables *in-line error handling*. When an error occurs, VBA will not notify the user of the error, but will otherwise act as if an error occurred, filling the Err object with information about the error. Execution then continues with the statement following the statement that caused the error. At this point, your code can use the Err object to determine which error has occurred and what to do about it.
On Error GoTo 0	Disables the error trap or in-line error handling. When an error occurs, VBA will return to its default error-handling behavior, which includes notifying the user of the error.

Example: The following function, DivideIt1, uses On Error Goto and an error trap to trap and handle errors:

```
Function DivideIt1(lngNum, lngDenom) As Variant
    On Error GoTo DivideIt1Error
    DivideIt1 = CDbl(lngNum) / CDbl(lngDenom)
DivideIt1Quit:
    On Error GoTo 0
Exit Function
DivideIt1Error:
    Select Case Err.Number
        Case 11
            MsgBox "Can't divide by zero"
        Case Else
            MsgBox "Unanticipated error"
    End Select
    DivideIt1 = Null
    Resume DivideIt1Quit
End Function
```

Notes: You can enable and disable an error handler and in-line error handling multiple times within a single procedure. A procedure, however, may only contain a single error trap.

Longer procedures are usually better served with an error trap rather than in-line error handling. In-line error handling, however, is useful for shorter procedures and procedures where you need to know exactly where to react differently based on where in the procedure the error has occurred.

When using an error trap, placing the trap at the end of the procedure and preceding the error trap with an Exit Function, Exit Sub, or Exit Property statement is a good idea, as shown in the DivideIt1 example, to prevent "falling into" the error handler.

Raise (Method)

Description: A method of the Err object used to generate a run-time error.

Syntax:

```
Err.Raise number [, source] [, description] [,
    helpfile] [, helpcontext]
```

Argument	Description
Err	The error object.
number	A Long between 0 and 65,535. When using Raise in a class module to raise a user-defined error, you should add vbObjectError to your error number.

Argument	Description
source	Optional. A string used to describe to VBA the source of the error. Defaults to the name of the VBA project.
description	Optional. A string that becomes the error message text. Defaults to either a built-in error message for VBA errors or "Application-defined or object-defined error" for user-defined errors.
helpfile	Optional. The fully-qualified path to the Windows Help file to associate with the error. Defaults to the VBA help file.
helpcontext	Optional. The context ID of the help topic in helpfile to associate with the error. If helpfile and helpcontext are specified, users may click on the Help button of the error dialog box to bring up context-sensitive help for the error. For existing VBA errors, defaults to the help text corresponding to the VBA error.

Example: The following raises a user-defined error with a custom error message and associated help:

```
Err.Raise 34566, "Invoice.Creation", _
  "You entered an illegal invoice number.", _
  "c:\inv\invoice.hlp", 250
```

Resume (Statement)

Description: Used inside of an error trap to redirect execution.

Syntax: There are three forms of the Resume statement:

Statement Form	Description
Resume [0]	Resumes execution at the statement that caused the error. Thus, VBA will attempt to re-execute the statement that caused the error. Use of the 0 parameter is optional and has no effect.
Resume Next	Resumes execution at the statement following the statement that caused the error. Thus, VBA will skip the statement that caused the error.
Resume line	Resumes execution at a specific statement. Line is a line number or label that points to a statement in the current procedure.

Example: This subroutine demonstrates the use of all three forms of the Resume statement:

```
Sub OpenFileOnDriveA(strFile As String)
    On Error GoTo OpenTrap

    Dim intResp As Integer
    Const errDriveNotReady = 71

    Open "a:\" & strFile For Random As 1
    MsgBox "Opened " & strFile
OpenQuit:
    On Error GoTo 0
    Exit Sub
OpenTrap:
    intResp = _
    MsgBox("Please insert disk into Drive A", _
        vbAbortRetryIgnore + vbCritical, _
        "OpenFileOnDriveA")
    Select Case intResp
    Case vbRetry
        Resume
    Case vbAbort
        Resume OpenQuit
    Case vbIgnore
        Resume Next
    End Select
End Sub
```

Notes: If you use the first form of the statement (Resume), you better fix the problem that caused the error. Otherwise, your program enters an endless loop.

Part VII

Files, Input, and Output

Your VBA host program most likely supports reading and writing files such as documents, spreadsheets, drawings, and databases. However, sometimes you just need to read or write data to a text or binary file. In these cases, the input and output functions and statements of VBA come in real handy. VBA includes many keywords—probably too many—for reading and writing data to and from files.

VBA also includes several keywords for managing disk files, directories, and folders. These statements and functions make it easy to get a list of files in a directory, or to copy, rename, or erase a file.

In this part . . .

✔ **Reading data from files**

✔ **Writing data to files**

✔ **Deleting files**

✔ **Managing files, directories, and folders**

✔ **Determining the length of a file**

✔ **Locking and unlocking files**

✔ **Getting a list of files in a directory**

Keyword Summary

Task	Keyword	Keyword Type
Close an open file	Close	Statement
Close all open files	Reset	Statement
Copy an unopened file	FileCopy	Statement
Delete an unopened file	Kill	Statement
Determine attributes of an unopened file, directory, or folder	GetAttr	Function
Determine if you have reached the end of a file	EOF	Function
Determine the date and time a file was last updated	FileDateTime	Function
Determine the file access mode for an open file	FileAttr	Function
Determine the length in bytes of an open file	LOF	Function
Determine the length in bytes of an unopened file	FileLen	Function
Determine the next file number available for use with the Open statement	FreeFile	Function
Determine the position of the next read/write file operation	Seek	Function
Determine the position of the previous read/write file operation	Loc	Function
Lock a portion of an open file	Lock	Statement
Open a file for processing	Open	Statement
Randomly read data from an open random or binary mode file	Get	Statement
Randomly write data to an open random or binary mode file	Put	Statement
Read a single line of data from an open sequential mode file	Line Input #	Statement
Read data from an open sequential mode file	Input #	Statement
Rename an unopened file, directory, or folder	Name	Statement
Return the names of files, directories, or folders	Dir	Function
Sequentially read data from an open input or binary mode file	Input	Function

Task	Keyword	Keyword Type
Set the attributes of an unopened file	SetAttr	Statement
Set the output width for a sequential text file	Width #	Statement
Set the position of the next read/write operation	Seek	Statement
Unlock a portion of a locked open file	Unlock	Statement
Write comma-delimited data to a text file	Write #	Statement
Write data to an open sequential mode file	Print #	Statement

Close (Statement)

Description: Closes a file opened using the Open statement.

Syntax:

```
Close [[#]filenumber1] [, [#]filenumber2] [,...]
```

Parameter	Description
filenumbers	Optional. A comma-delimited list of one or more file numbers. If omitted, Close closes all files that were opened using the Open statement. The pound sign (#) preceding each file number is optional.

Example: This closes file number 1:

```
Close #1 ' Close 1 is equivalent
```

This closes all open files:

```
Close
```

Dir (Function)

Description: Returns a String containing the name of a file, directory, or folder matching a specified filter or list of attributes.

Syntax:

```
Dir[( pathname [, attributes] )]
```

Argument	Description
`pathname`	A string that specifies a file, directory, or folder. May include wildcard characters. The first time you call `Dir`, pathname is required; on subsequent calls, you must omit the pathname. (*See also* Notes section for more details.)
`attributes`	Optional. One or more constants that specify attributes for the file, directory, or folders returned by `Dir`. If you wish to use more than one constant, you add them together. May be one of the following constants:

Constant	Value	Description
`vbNormal`	0	Includes normal (non-hidden, non-system, non-directory) files. The default.
`vbHidden`	2	Also includes hidden files.
`vbSystem`	4	Also includes system files.
`vbVolume`	8	Includes only the volume label; if specified, VBA disregards all other attributes.
`vbDirectory`	16	Also includes directory or folders.

Example: This subroutine prints all files matching the strPath file specification to the Immediate window:

```
Sub ListFiles(strPath As String)
    Dim strFile As String
    Dim intCount As Integer

    intCount = 0
    strFile = Dir(strPath)
    Do While strFile <> ""
        Debug.Print strFile
        intCount = intCount + 1
        strFile = Dir
    Loop
    Debug.Print "Total of " & intCount & " files
    listed."
End Sub
```

Notes: `Dir` is a strange but useful function. The first time you call it, you must supply a pathname and an optional set of attributes. `Dir` returns the first file, directory, or folder that meets the specified parameters. Thereafter, you call `Dir` repeatedly without any parameters (or even the parentheses), and it supplies the next file, directory, or folder that meets the original pathname and attributes. When no more file, directory, or folders are found, `Dir` returns a zero-length string.

When you set attributes to `vbHidden`, `vbSystem`, or `vbDirectory` (or a combination of these), normal files are not excluded. If you wish to exclude normal files, you must use the

GetAttr function to check the attributes of the returned files.
(**See also** the definition of GetAttr in this part for an example of
how to do this.)

EOF (Function)

Description: Returns True when the end of the file that was
opened for sequential or random input has been reached.

Syntax:

EOF (*filenumber*)

Argument	Description
filenumber	An Integer value specifying the file number of an open file.

Example: This code opens a file and reads and prints each line of
the file until EOF is reached:

```
Open "c:\dummies\test.txt" For Input As #1
Do While Not EOF(1)
    Line Input #1, strLine
    Debug.Print strLine
Loop
Close #1
```

Notes: For files opened for sequential input, EOF returns True
when the end of file has been reached. For files opened for random
or binary input, EOF returns True when a Get statement is unable
to read an entire record. For files opened for output, EOF always
returns True.

FileAttr (Function)

Description: Returns a Long number corresponding to the file
access mode that the open file uses.

Syntax:

FileAttr (*filenumber*, *returntype*)

Argument	Description
filenumber	An Integer designating a valid file number.
returntype	An Integer designating the type of information FileAttr should return. May be one of the following values:

Value	Description
1	Returns a value indicating the file access mode.
2	Returns an operating system file handle to the file. (16-bit operating systems only; this causes an error when used on 32-bit operating systems.)

When a returntype of 1 is used, FileAttr returns one of the following values:

Return Value	Description
1	Input
2	Output
4	Random
8	Append
32	Binary

Example:

```
Open "c:\dummies\test.txt" For Binary As #1
lngFA = FileAttr(1, 1) '= 32
```

FileCopy (Statement)

Description: Copies an unopened file.

Syntax:

```
FileCopy source, destination
```

Argument	Description
source	A String containing the name of the file to be copied.
destination	A String containing the name of the destination file.

Example:

```
FileCopy "c:\dummies\test.txt", "a:\test.txt"
```

Notes: Unlike the DOS copy command, the destination argument must include a filename or an error will occur.

FileDateTime (Function)

Description: Returns a Variant of the Date subtype equal to the date and time the file was last modified.

Syntax:

```
FileDateTime( pathname )
```

Argument	Description
pathname	A string containing the complete path to a file, directory, or folder.

Example: In the following code, datLtr will be equal to the date and time the file was last modified (like "4/24/98 4:39:28 PM"):

```
datLtr = FileDateTime("d:\wp\letter.doc")
```

FileLen (Function)

Description: Returns the size of a file in bytes.

Syntax:

```
FileLen ( pathname )
```

Argument	Description
pathname	A string containing the complete path to a file, directory, or folder.

Example: If autoexec.bat is 125 bytes long, lngLength would equal 125:

```
lngLength = FileLen("c:\autoexec.bat")
```

Notes: If you have the file open, FileLen returns the size of the file before it was opened. If you need to determine the length of the open file, use the LOF function instead.

FreeFile (Function)

Description: Returns an Integer containing the next available file number for use with the Open statement.

Syntax:

```
FreeFile [( rangenumber )]
```

Argument	Description
rangenumber	Optional. A Variant that specifies the range of free file numbers that FreeFile should use. Can be 0 (the default) to indicate that FreeFile should return a free

Argument	Description
	file number in the range of 1-255 or 1 to indicate that FreeFile should return a free file number in the range of 256-511.

Example:

```
intFN = FreeFile
Open "c:\dummies\test.txt" For Input As intFN
```

Notes: Using FreeFile before any Open statement is always a good idea because you don't really care about which file number you use, just that it doesn't conflict with any other open file's file number.

Get (Statement)

Description: Reads data from a file opened in random or binary access mode.

Syntax:

```
Get [#]filenumber [, recnumber], varname
```

Argument	Description
filenumber	An Integer value specifying the file number of an open file. The preceding pound sign character (#) is optional.
recnumber	Optional. The position in the file from which to begin reading. For random mode files, this is the record number. For binary mode files, this is the byte number. Defaults to the next position in the file.
varname	The name of a variable into which Get places the data.

Example: This example reads records from a random access file. The records were previously written to this file using Put statements and the Grail user-defined Type. (*See also* the example following the definition of the Put statement.):

```
'Place this Type definition in the
'Declarations section of a module.
Type Grail
    strName As String * 30
    strQuest As String * 50
    strOther As String * 30
End Type

Sub FileGet()
    Dim intFN As Integer
```

```
Dim recBridgeCrossing As Grail
Dim intCount As Integer

intFN = FreeFile
intCount = 0
Open "c:\dummies\test.rnd" For Random As intFN _
  Len = Len(recBridgeCrossing)
Do While Not EOF(intFN)
    intCount = intCount + 1
    Get intFN, , recBridgeCrossing
    With recBridgeCrossing
        Debug.Print "#" & intCount & _
        ", Name: " & Trim(.strName) & _
        ", Quest: " & Trim(.strQuest) & _
        ", Other: " & Trim(.strOther)
    End With
Loop
Close intFN
End Sub
```

Notes: Data read with the Get statement is best written with the Put statement.

Using "Len = Len(reclength)" with random access files is a good idea (when reading data from binary access mode files, the Len clause is ignored). If you don't use the Len argument when outputting data that uses Put statements, VBA creates records that exceed the length of your records. This messes you up when you later use Get to read the data.

GetAttr (Function)

Description: Returns an Integer number indicating the file attributes of a file.

Syntax:

GetAttr(*pathname*)

Argument	Description
pathname	A string containing the complete path to a file, directory, or folder.

GetAttr returns a number that is the sum of the following file attribute constants:

Constant	Value	Description
vbNormal	0	Normal file without any special attributes.
vbReadOnly	1	Read only file.

Constant	Value	Description
vbHidden	2	Hidden file.
vbSystem	4	System file (not valid on Macintosh).
vbDirectory	16	Directory or folder.
vbArchive	32	File has changed since last backup (not valid on Macintosh).
vbAlias	64	Macintosh alias (not valid on non-Macintoshes).

Example: This sample function returns True if the file has the specified attribute set:

```
Function IsAttributeSet(strFile As String, _
  intAttribute As Integer) As Boolean
    IsAttributeSet = (GetAttr(strFile) _
    And intAttribute) = intAttribute
End Function
```

Notes: Because the return value of GetAttr is the sum of file attributes of the file, you must use *bitwise arithmetic* to determine whether a specific attribute (or bit) is set. All this means is that you need to apply some math magic to the returned value so it only displays the bit you're interested in. In this case, you use the And operator to mask off the individual file attribute. For example, you can use the following code to determine if a file is a system file:

```
fSet1 = GetAttr("c:\msdos.sys") And vbSystem
```

In the above, fSet1 will returns 0 if c:\msdos.sys is a non-system file, or a non-zero value if it's a system file.

Input (Function)

Description: Returns a String containing a sequentially read number of characters from a file that has been opened in input or binary mode.

Syntax:

Input(*number*, [#]*filenumber*)

Argument	Description
number	The number of characters to read from the file. Input begins reading the data one character after the last character read.
filenumber	An Integer value specifying the file number of an open file. The preceding pound sign character (#) is optional.

Example: This code reads and prints to the Immediate window each character from test.txt on a separate line:

```
intFN = FreeFile
Open "c:\dummies\test.txt" For Input As intFN
Do While Not EOF(intFN)
    'read the next character in the file
    strInput = Input(1, intFN)
    Debug.Print strInput
Loop
```

Notes: The Input function works only with files opened in input or binary modes. Unlike the Input # statement, the Input function reads all characters, including line feed and carriage return characters, delimiters, and spaces.

The Input function is best used with sequential text data written to the file using the Print # statement.

Input # (Statement)

Description: Reads data from a comma-delimited text file that has been opened in input or binary mode.

Syntax:

Input #*filenumber*, *varlist*

Argument	Description
filenumber	An Integer value specifying the file number of an open file. The preceding pound sign character (#) is *required*.
varlist	Comma-delimited list of variables in which the data is to be read.

Example: This code reads through a delimited text file until it reaches the end of the file:

```
intFN = FreeFile
Open "c:\dummies\delim.txt" _
 For Input As intFN
Do While Not EOF(intFN)
    Input #intFN, varFirstName, varLastName,
    varPhone
    Debug.Print varFirstName, varLastName, varPhone
Loop
```

Notes: The Input # statement works only with files opened in input or binary modes. Unlike the Input function, the Input # statement doesn't actually read line feed and carriage return characters, delimiters, and spaces. Instead, the Input # statement uses these characters for positioning.

The Input # statement is best used with sequential text data written to the file using the Write # statement. Make sure your Input # statement's variable list matches the output list used in the corresponding Write # statement.

Kill (Statement)

Description: Deletes an unopened file.

Syntax:

Kill *pathname*

Argument	Description
pathname	A string containing the complete path to one or more files.

Example: This statement permanently deletes the deleteme.txt file:

Kill "c:\dummies\deleteme.txt"

Notes: If you need to delete a directory or folder, use the RmDir statement.

Line Input # (Statement)

Description: Reads a single line of data from a sequential text file that has been opened in input or binary mode.

Syntax:

Line Input #*filenumber*, *varname*

Argument	Description
filenumber	An Integer value specifying the file number of an open file. The preceding pound sign character (#) is *required*.
varlist	A variable of the String or Variant datatype into which the data is to be read.

Example: This example reads lines of text from the test.txt file and prints them to the Immediate window:

```
intFN = FreeFile
Open "c:\dummies\test.txt" For Input As intFN
Do While Not EOF(intFN)
    Line Input #intFN, varLine
    Debug.Print varLine
Loop
```

Notes: The Line Input # statement works only with files opened in input mode. It reads all data on a line until a carriage-return character or carriage-return-linefeed sequence. The carriage-return and linefeed characters are not read into the variable.

The Line Input # statement is best used with sequential text data written to the file using the Print # statement.

Loc (Function)

Description: Returns a Long containing the position in the file of the most recent read/write operation.

Syntax:

Loc(*filenumber*)

Argument	Description
filenumber	An Integer value specifying the file number of an open file.

The value returned by Loc depends upon the access mode of the file:

Mode	Loc returns
Random	Record number of previously read or written record.
Sequential	Byte position of the previously read or written data item divided by 128.
Binary	Position of the last byte read or written.

Example:

```
Open "c:\dummies\test2.rnd" _
 For Random As #1 Len=20
IngLoc=Loc(1)
```

Lock (Statement)

Description: Locks a portion of an open file.

Syntax:

Lock [#]*filenumber*, [*recordrange*]

Argument	Description
filenumber	An Integer value specifying the file number of an open file. The preceding pound sign character (#) is optional.
recordrange	Optional. The range of records to lock. Defaults to the entire file. Recordrange can be a single record or a range of records of the form "[*start*] To *end*".

Example: This example locks record #5, writes to the record using Put, and then releases the lock:

```
Lock intFN, 5
Put intFN, 5, strName
Unlock intFN, 5
```

Notes: Use the Lock and Unlock statements when writing to shared data files. Pair the Lock statement with an Unlock statement that unlocks the same record(s) after the write operation has been performed.

LOF (Function)

Description: Returns a Long containing the length in bytes of an open file.

Syntax:

```
LOF( filenumber )
```

Argument	Description
filenumber	An Integer value specifying the file number of an open file.

Example: At the end of this example, lngLength will equal the length of test.rnd in bytes:

```
intFN = FreeFile
Open "c:\dummies\test.rnd" For Random As intFN _
 Len = Len(strName)
lngLength = LOF(intFN)
```

Name (Statement)

Description: Renames or moves an unopened file, directory, or folder.

Syntax:

```
Name oldpathname As newpathname
```

Argument	Description
oldpathname	A string containing the complete path to an existing file, directory, or folder.
newpathname	A string containing the complete path to the renamed file, directory, or folder. newpathname must not already exist.

Example: This code renames test.txt to invoice.txt:

```
Name "c:\vba\test.txt" As
    "c:\vba\invoice.txt"
```

Notes: If the path of newpathname differs from the path of oldpathname, Rename moves the file.

Unlike the DOS rename command, you need to specify the complete path to the new file if you wish only to rename it. If you don't, the file moves to the default directory.

Open (Statement)

Description: Opens a file for processing.

Syntax:

```
Open pathname [For mode] [Access access] [lock] As
    [#]filenumber [Len=reclength]
```

Argument	Description
pathname	A string containing the complete path to a file.
mode	Optional. Keyword used to specify the file access mode (see below). Defaults to Random.
access	Optional. Keyword used to specify the permissible operations. Can be Read, Write, or Read Write. Defaults to Read Write. Ignored if the file is opened in Append, Input, or Output modes.
lock	Optional. Keyword used to specify how the file is to be shared with other processes. Can be Shared, Lock Read, Lock Write, Lock Read Write. Defaults to Shared.
filenumber	An Integer value specifying the file number of an open file. The preceding pound sign character (#) is optional.
reclength	Optional. Integer from 1 to 32,767 indicating the record length for files opened in random mode. For sequential files, this value determines the length of the read/write buffer. For binary mode, this value is ignored.

Mode can be any of the following:

Keyword	Description
Append	Opens an existing sequential text file for appended output. If the file doesn't already exist, it's created; if the file already exists, data is appended to it.
Binary	Opens a binary file for input or output. If the file doesn't already exist, it's created.
Input	Opens an existing sequential text file for input. An error occurs if the file doesn't already exist.
Output	Opens a new sequential text file for output. If the file doesn't already exist, it's created; if the file already exists, it's replaced.
Random	Opens a text file for record-oriented input or output. If the file doesn't already exist, it's created.

Example: This code opens a file for sequential input:

```
Open "c:\vba\text.txt" For Input As #1
```

This code opens a file for sequential output; data is appended to any existing file:

```
Open "c:\vba\text.txt" For Append As #3
```

This code opens a file in the random mode with a record length of 50:

```
Open "c:\vba\random.txt" For Random As #4 Len=50
```

Notes: Unlike most VBA statements and functions, the Open statement uses neither positional nor named parameters. Instead it uses a special hybrid syntax.

Use the FreeFile function to determine the next available file number. *See also* the definition of FreeFile.

Print # (Statement)

Description: Writes data to an open sequential file.

Syntax:

```
Print #filenumber [, outputlist]
```

Argument	Description
filenumber	An Integer value specifying the file number of an open file. The preceding pound sign character (#) is *required*.

Argument	Description
outputlist	Optional. One or more output expressions. If omitted, a blank line is written to the file. Each item in the outputlist is made up of an expression you wish to print, and a delimiting character, which may be a comma or a semicolon. If you use a comma, VBA skips to the next print location. Print locations occur every 14 characters. If you use a semicolon, the item prints in the next column. Items may be separated with Spc(n) or Tab(n). Spc(n) causes Print # to skip n spaces before printing the next item. Tab(n) causes Print # to skip to the nth column of the line, unless the current column is greater than n, in which case, Print # skips to the nth column of the next line.

Example: This statement prints "hello", skips to next print position, and then prints "there":

```
Print #intFN, "hello, "there"
```

This statement prints "hello", skips to column 20, and then prints "there":

```
Print #intFN, "hello"; Tab(20); "there"
```

Notes: If you need to create fixed width text files, use Print #. However, if you need to create delimited text files, the Write # statement is a better choice.

Put (Statement)

Description: Writes data to a file opened in random or binary access mode.

Syntax:

```
Put [#]filenumber [, recnumber], varname
```

Argument	Description
filenumber	An integer value specifying the file number of an open file. The preceding pound sign character (#) is optional.
recnumber	Optional. The position in the file at which the data is to be written. For random mode files, this is the record number. For binary mode files, this is the byte number. Defaults to the next position in the file. For existing files, Put overwrites existing records unless you use a record number greater than any existing records.
varname	The name of a variable from which Put reads the data.

Example: The following example writes records to a random access using the Grail user-defined Type. (*See also* the example under the Get statement.)

```
Sub FilePut()
    Dim intFN As Integer
    Dim recBridgeCrossing As Grail

    intFN = FreeFile
    Open "c:\dummies\test.rnd" _
     For Random As intFN _
     Len = Len(recBridgeCrossing)

    With recBridgeCrossing
        .strName = "Sir Robin"
        .strQuest = "To seek the holy grail"
        .strOther = "Blue"
        End With
    'write the recBridgeCrossing values to
    'the 10th record
    Put #intFN, 10, recBridgeCrossing
    Close intFN
End Sub
```

Notes: Data written with the Put statement is best read with the Get statement.

Reset (Statement)

Description: Closes all files that have been opened with the Open statement.

Syntax:

Reset

Example:

Reset

Notes: If any file buffers have not been written to disk, Reset first writes the unsaved buffers before closing files.

If you need to close a single file, use the Close statement instead.

Seek (Function)

Description: Returns the position of the next read/write file operation.

Syntax:

Seek(*filenumber*)

Argument	Description
filenumber	An Integer value specifying the file number of an open file.

Example: This example, opens a file in Append mode, writes several variables to the file and then uses the Seek function to determine the current position in the opened file:

```
intFN = FreeFile
Open "c:\dummies\delim1.txt" _
 For Append As intFN
varFirstName = "Joe"
varLastName = "Smith"
Write #intFN, varFirstName, varLastName
lngBytePos = Seek(intFN) '= 46
```

Notes: For random access mode files, Seek returns the record number of the next read/write file operation. For all other access modes, Seek returns the byte number.

Seek (Statement)

Description: Sets the position of the next read/write operation.

Syntax:

Seek [#]*filenumber, position*

Argument	Description
filenumber	An Integer value specifying the file number of an open file. The preceding pound sign character (#) is optional.
position	The position in the file at which the next read/write operation should occur. For random mode files, this is the record number. For all other access modes, this is the byte number.

Example: This example reads only the thirteenth record from a random access file by using the Seek statement prior to the Get statement. The records were previously written to this file using Put statements and the Grail user-defined Type (*See also* the example following the definition of the Put statement.):

```
    intFN = FreeFile
    Open "c:\dummies\test.rnd" For Random As intFN _
    Len = Len(recBridgeCrossing)
    'move to record 13
    Seek intFN, 13
    Get intFN, , recBridgeCrossing
```

Notes: The Seek statement is primarily used with Random mode files.

SetAttr (Statement)

Description: Sets the attributes of an unopened file.

Syntax:

SetAttr *pathname, attributes*

Argument	Description
pathname	A string containing the complete path to a file, directory, or folder.
attributes	A constant specifying the attribute or attributes to set for the file, directory, or folder. Can be one or more of the attribute constants described under the GetAttr function (if you want to set multiple attributes, add the constants together):

Example: This example makes a file read only:

SetAttr "c:\dummies\data.txt", vbReadOnly

This example makes a file both system and hidden:

SetAttr "c:\driver.sys", vbHidden + vbSystem

Notes: To determine the file attributes of an existing file, you use the GetAttr function.

Unlock (Statement)

Description: Unlocks a portion of an open file that has been locked using the Lock statement.

Syntax:

Unlock [#]*filenumber* [, *recordrange*]

Argument	Description
filenumber	An integer value specifying the file number of an open file. The preceding pound sign character (#) is optional.

Argument	Description
recordrange	Optional. The range of records to unlock. Defaults to the entire file. Recordrange can be a single record or a range of records of the form "[start] To end".

Example: See the example under the Lock statement.

Width # (Statement)

Description: Sets the output width for a sequential text file.

Syntax:

```
Width #filenumber, width
```

Argument	Description
filenumber	An Integer value specifying the file number of an open file. The preceding pound sign character (#) is *required*.
width	A number indicating the width of a line in the file. Can be between 0 and 255. If set to 0, there is no limit to the width of the file.

Example: In this example, strText1 is written to line 1 of the file and strText2 is written to line 2:

```
Open "c:\dummies\test.txt" _
 For Append As intFN
strText1 = "This is a long string"
strText2 = "Another one"
Width #intFN, 10
Print #intFN, strText1; strText2
```

Notes: For data written using the Print # statement, any data that exceeds the width of the file is wrapped around to the next line, but only at field breaks. Thus, in the example, "This is a long string" would print on one line, with "Another one" printed on the second line.

For data written using the Write # statement, the width specified with the Width # statement is ignored.

Write # (Statement)

Description: Writes comma-delimited data to a sequential text file.

Syntax:

```
Write #filenumber [, outputlist]
```

Argument	Description
filenumber	An Integer value specifying the file number of an open file. The preceding pound sign character (#) is *required*.
outputlist	Optional. Comma-delimited list of expressions to write to the file. If omitted, a blank file is written to the file.

Example: This code writes three comma-delimited records to a sequential text file:

```
intFN = FreeFile
Open "c:\dummies\delim.txt" _
  For Output As intFN
Write #intFN, "Joe", "Smith", "English Teacher", 1
Write #intFN, "Geoff", "Litwin", "Student", 2
Write #intFN, "Alicia", "Comstock", "Writer", 3
```

Notes: The Write # statement only works with files opened in output or append modes. Unlike the Print # function, the Write # statement separates values using commas and wraps strings with double quotes.

The following values are treated specially by the Write # statement:

Value of variable	Value written
Empty	*nothing*
Null	#NULL#
True or False	#TRUE# or #FALSE#
Date or time	#yyyy-mm-dd hh:mm:ss#
Variant of the Error subtype	#ERROR errornumber#

Data written using the Write # statement is best read with the Input # statement. Make sure your Input # statement's variable list matches the output list used in the Write # statement.

Part VIII

Looping and Branching

Almost every VBA procedure you write will include some form of branching or looping. It's hard to do much without using an If...Then statement or a Do While loop. There's lots of looping and branching statements to choose from. In addition, you can use the IIf function and several related functions to branch right within an expression. Sort of like a mini-VBA program you can use within an Excel cell or perhaps an Access query.

In this part . . .

- ✔ Branching based on a condition

- ✔ Repeatedly executing a series of statements

- ✔ Unconditionally jumping to a line number or label

- ✔ Returning a value based on the value of an index

- ✔ Iterating through the items in a collection or an array

- ✔ Pausing the execution of a procedure

Keyword Summary

Task	Keyword	Keyword Type
Conditionally execute one of several groups of statements based on the value of a single condition	Select Case	Statement
Conditionally execute one or more groups of statements based on the value of one or more conditions	If...Then...Else	Statement
Efficiently execute a block of statements against an object or user-defined type	With...End With	Statement
Iterate through the items in a collection or an array	For Each...Next	Statement
Jump to a label or line number in a procedure based on a condition	On...GoTo	Statement
Jump to a label or line number in a procedure	GoTo	Statement
Jump to a part of a procedure and return when done	GoSub...Return	Statement
Jump to a part of a procedure based on a condition	On...GoSub	Statement
Loop through a block of statements while a condition is true	While...Wend	Statement
Loop through a block of statements while incrementing a counter	For...Next	Statement
Loop through a block of statements while or until a condition is true	Do...Loop	Statement
Pause the execution of a procedure	Stop	Statement
Return a value from a series of values based on the truth of a corresponding series of conditions	Switch	Function
Return one of several values based on the value of an index	Choose	Function

Task	Keyword	Keyword Type
Return one of two values based on a condition	IIf	Function
Return the position of a value within a segmented range of values	Partition	Function
Terminate execution and reset all variables	End	Statement

Choose (Function)

Description: Returns one of several values based on the value of an index.

Syntax:

```
Choose( index, choice-1 [, choice-2],…[, choice-n])
```

Argument	Description
index	A number between 1 and the number of choices.
choice	A Variant expression to return if index is the same as the position of this item in the list. The counting of items starts with 1, so that choice-1 is returned if index is 1, choice-2 is returned if index is 2, and so forth.

Example:

```
intGender = 2
varGender = Choose(intGender, "M", "F") '="F"
```

Notes: If index is not a whole number, it is truncated to a whole number before making a choice. If index is less than 1 or exceeds the number of choices, a Null is returned by Choose.

All the choices are evaluated by Choose, no matter which one is returned. Thus, don't use expressions like MsgBox, whose unintended evaluation could be a problem.

Do...Loop (Statement)

Description: Loops through a block of statements while or until a condition is true.

Syntax: There are two forms of the Do...Loop statement. In the first form, the condition is evaluated at the top of the loop:

```
Do [{While | Until} condition]
    [statements]
    [Exit Do]
    [statements]
Loop
```

In the second form of Do...Loop, the condition is evaluated at the bottom of the loop. This ensures that the statements inside the loop are executed at least once:

```
Do
    [statements]
    [Exit Do]
    [statements]
Loop  [{While | Until} condition]
```

Argument	Description
condition	Optional. An expression that evaluates to True or False. If preceded by While, the statements in the loop are executed while the condition is True. If preceded by Until, the statements are executed until the condition is True. If no condition is specified, the statements in the loop are executed repeatedly; the loop can only be exited using the Exit Do statement.
statements	Optional. One or more statements. If omitted, the loop will be endless.

Example: The following function, ReverseIt, reverses the characters in a string, making use of a Do...Loop statement in the process (for example, ReverseIt("hello") = "olleh"):

```
Function ReverseIt(ByVal strStr As String) As
    String
    'Reverses the characters in a string
    Dim strReverse As String
    Do While Len(strStr) > 0
        strReverse = strReverse + Right(strStr, 1)
    strStr = Left(strStr, Len(strStr) - 1)
    Loop
    ReverseIt = strReverse
End Function
```

Notes: If the condition evaluates to Null, the condition is treated as False.

End (Statement)

Description: Terminates execution and resets all variables.

Syntax:

```
End
```

Example:

```
End
```

Notes: The End statement completely terminates execution of the program; if you wish to pause the program use the Stop statement or a breakpoint instead.

For Each...Next (Statement)

Description: Iterates through the items in a collection or an array.

Syntax:

```
For Each element In group
    [statements]
    [Exit For]
    [statements]
Next [element]
```

Argument	Description
element	Variable used to iterate through the collection or array. For arrays, element must be a Variant. For collections, element may be a Variant or an Object variable.
group	Name of object collection or array.
statements	Optional. One or more statements. If omitted, the loop won't actually do anything.

Example: This example prints to the Immediate window all of the items in the colFruit collection:

```
Dim colFruit As New Collection
Dim varItem As Variant
'...
For Each varItem In colFruit
    Debug.Print varItem
Next varItem
```

This example prints to the Immediate window each element of the avarAges array:

```
Dim varItem As Variant
Dim avarAges(1 To 10) As Integer
'...
For Each varItem In avarAges()
    Debug.Print varItem
Next varItem
```

Notes: When iterating through collections or arrays, For
Each...Next is more efficient than For...Next. You can't use
For Each...Next, however, if you need to modify the item value.

For...Next (Statement)

Description: Loops through a block of statements while
incrementing a counter.

Syntax:

```
For counter = start To end [Step step]
    [statements]
    [Exit For]
    [statements]
Next [counter]
```

Argument	Description
counter	A numeric or Variant variable used as a loop counter.
start	The starting value for counter. A number.
end	The ending value for counter. A number.
step	Optional. The increment added to counter for each iteration of the loop. Defaults to 1.
statements	Optional. One or more statements. If omitted, the loop won't actually do anything.

Example: This trivial function sums all of the numbers between
two values, making use of a For...Next statement in the process:

```
Function AddEmUp(intLower As Integer, _
  intUpper As Integer) As Long
    Dim lngSum As Long
    Dim intCount As Integer
    lngSum = 0
    For intCount = intLower To intUpper
        lngSum = lngSum + intCount
    Next intCount
    AddEmUp = lngSum
End Function
```

Notes: Step may be a positive or negative value. If start is less
than end and step is not a negative value, the statements in the
loop are never executed. Similarly, if start is greater than end
and step is negative, the statements are never executed.

GoSub...Return (Statement)

Description: Jumps to a part of a procedure — defined by a line number or label — and returns when done.

Syntax:

```
GoSub line_number_or_label
'...
line
'...
Return
```

Argument	Description
line_number_or_label	The number of a line or a line label.
line	A line of code identified by either a line number or a statement label.

Example: Here's a trivial example of using GoSub...Return (this could have been better handled with an If...Then statement):

```
Function Divide1(intNum As Integer, _
  intDenom As Integer) As Double
    If intDenom = 0 Then GoSub DivideByZero
    Divide1 = intNum / intDenom
    Exit Function
DivideByZero:
    intNum = 0
    intDenom = 1
    Return
End Function
```

Notes: The GoSub. . .Return statement is an older part of VBA that is usually best avoided. You can usually replace code that employs GoSub with an If. . .Then. . .Else statement or you might break up a procedure that employs GoSub into multiple procedures.

GoTo (Statement)

Description: Jumps to a label or line number in a procedure.

Syntax:

```
GoTo line_number_or_label
'...
line
'...
```

Argument	Description
line_number_or_label	The number of a line or a line label.
line	A line of code identified by either a line number or a statement label.

Example: This function uses GoTo to avoid division by zero:

```
Function Divide2(intNum As Integer, _
  intDenom As Integer) As Double
    If intDenom = 0 Then GoTo Divide2Quit
    Divide2 = intNum / intDenom
Divide2Quit:
End Function
```

Notes: If possible, avoid using GoTo. Use If...Then...Else instead.

If...Then...Else (Statement)

Description: Executes one or more groups of statements based on the value of one or more conditions.

Syntax: VBA has two forms of the If...Then...Else statement, the in-line version ...

```
If condition Then [statements] [Else elsestatement]
```

... or the block version:

```
If condition Then
    [statements]
[ElseIf condition-1 Then
    [elseifstatements]]
    ...
[ElseIf condition-n Then
    [elseifstatements]]
[Else
    [elsestatements]]
EndIf
```

Argument	Description
condition	An expression that evaluates to True or False. If the expression is Null, VBA treats the expression as if it were False.
statements	Optional. One or more statements to execute if the condition is True.
elseifstatements	Optional. One or more statements to execute if the associated condition-n is True.
elsestatements	Optional. One of more statements to execute if no other condition is True.

Example: This function returns a `String` corresponding to an `Integer` value for season:

```
Function SeasonString(intSeason As Integer) As
    String
    If intSeason = 1 Then
        SeasonString = "Winter"
    ElseIf intSeason = 2 Then
        SeasonString = "Spring"
    ElseIf intSeason = 3 Then
        SeasonString = "Summer"
    ElseIf intSeason = 4 Then
        SeasonString = "Fall"
    Else
        SeasonString = ""
    End If
End Function
```

Notes: By using the `ElseIf` clause, you can often avoid having to use nested `If...Then...Else` statements.

If you have more than two groups of statements and their conditions evaluate the same expression against a list of values, using `Select...Case` is more efficient. On the other hand, if you need to evaluate different expressions, use the `If...Then...Else` statement.

IIf (Function)

Description: Returns one of two values based on a condition.

Syntax:

```
IIf( expr, truepart, falsepart )
```

Argument	Description
expr	An expression that evaluates to `True` or `False`. If the expression is `Null`, VBA treats the expression as if it were `False`.
truepart	The value or expression to return if `expr` is `True`.
falsepart	The value or expression to return if `expr` is `False`.

Example:

```
intSex = 1
strSex = IIf(intSex = 1, "Male", "Female") '= Male
```

> **Notes:** Both truepart and falsepart are evaluated by IIf regardless of the truth of the expression, so don't include functions such as MsgBox in the truepart or falsepart expressions.

Partition (Function)

Description: Returns the position of a value within a segmented range of values.

Syntax:

Partition(number, start, stop, interval)

Argument	Description
number	A number to check against a range of values. If number is a floating-point number, it is rounded before being evaluated.
start	A number designating the lower bound of the range. If start is a floating-point number, it is rounded before being evaluated. Start can't be less than 0.
stop	A number designating the upper bound of the range. If stop is a floating-point number, it is rounded before being evaluated. Stop must be greater than start.
interval	A number indicating the number of intervals in which to divide up the range. The length of each interval equals (stop-start+1)/interval.

Partition returns a Variant of the String subtype identifying the interval in the following format:

interval_begin: *interval_end*

Both interval_begin and interval_end are padded with leading blanks.

If the number is less than start or greater than stop, Partition returns " :start-1" or "stop+1: ", respectively.

If any of the arguments are Null, Partition returns Null.

Example:

varRet = Partition(10, 1, 10000, 1000)'= 1: 1000

Select Case (Statement)

Description: Executes one of several groups of statements based on the value of a single condition.

Syntax:

```
Select Case testexpression
    [Case expressionlist-1]
        [statements-1]]
    '...
    [Case expressionlist-n]
        [statements-n]]
    [Case Else
        [elsestatements]]
End Select
```

Argument	Description
testexpression	An expression that evaluates to a string or number.
expressionlist-n	Optional. A value or list of values to compare with testexpression. If testexpression is equal to the expressionlist, the statements associated with the Case clause are executed. Expressionlist may contain a simple value ("a"), a range of values (9 to 15), or the keyword Is with a comparison operator (Is < 9). You can't use the Like or Between operators in an expressionlist.
statements-n	Optional. One or more statements to execute if testexpression matches the associated Case clause.
elsestatements	Optional. One or more statements to execute if testexpression doesn't match any of the expressionlists associated with Case clause.

Example: This function determines the type of character that is passed to it, making use of a Select Case statement in the process:

```
Function CharType(strChar As String) As String
    Select Case Left(strChar, 1)
        Case "a" To "z", "A" To "Z"
            CharType = "Alphabet"
        Case "0" To "9"
            CharType = "Number"
        Case ".", ",", "?", ";", ":", "!"
            CharType = "Punctuation"
        Case Else
            CharType = "Other"
    End Select
End Function
```

Notes: Use an Else clause to handle data that doesn't fall into any of the other cases.

Stop (Statement)

Description: Pauses the execution of a procedure and places VBA in break mode.

Syntax:

```
Stop
```

Example:

```
Stop
```

Notes: While in break mode, you can examine the contents of variables using the Immediate or Locals windows, set or view watch expressions, or single-step through your code using one of the Debug menu commands. You can resume execution of the procedure by choosing the Run⇨Continue menu command.

Using the Stop statement is equivalent to setting a breakpoint in your code.

Switch (Function)

Description: Returns a value from a series of values based on the truth of a corresponding series of conditions.

Syntax:

```
Switch( expr-1, value-1 [, expr-2, value-2,
    [..., expr-n, value-n]])
```

Argument	Description
expr	An expression that evaluates to True or False.
value	A value to return if the corresponding expression is True.

Example: In this example, varRet will equal 'Minor' because 'intAge<21' is evaluated before 'strSex="F"':

```
intAge = 20
strSex = "F"
varRet = Switch(intAge < 21, "Minor", _
  strSex = "F", "Female Adult", strSex = "M", _
  "Male Adult")
```

Notes: If multiple expressions are True, Switch returns the first value where the expression is True (see the example). If none of the expressions are True, Switch returns Null.

The choices are all evaluated by Switch, no matter which one is returned. Thus, it's important not to use expressions like MsgBox whose unintended evaluation could be a problem.

While...Wend (Statement)

Description: Loops through a block of statements while a condition is true.

Syntax:

```
While condition
    [statements]
Wend
```

Argument	Description
condition	An expression that evaluates to True or False. If Null, the expression is treated as if it were False.
statements	Optional. One or more statements to execute while condition is True.

Example: This code prints the numbers from 1 and 10 to the Immediate window.

```
intCount = 1
While intCount <= 10
    Debug.Print intCount
    intCount = intCount + 1
Wend
```

Notes: The Do While...Loop statement is more flexible than the While...Wend statement. Therefore, in general, you should use Do While...Loop instead of While...Wend.

With...End With (Statement)

Description: Efficiently executes a block of statements against an object or user-defined type.

Syntax:

```
With object
    [statements]
End With
```

Argument	Description
object	A reference to an object, an object variable, or a user-defined type variable.
statements	Optional. One or more statements that reference object. (You may also include here statements that do not reference object.)

Example: This example adds items to the colFruits collection without having to repeatedly refer to the collection:

```
Dim colFruit As New Collection
With colFruit
    .Add "apple"
    .Add "peach"
    .Add "pear"
End With
```

Notes: While you may nest With...End With statements, code in the nested statement block only sees the inner-most object. In order to reference objects in outer blocks, you must fully qualify your object references.

Part IX

Mathematical and Financial Operations

Mathematics and accounting — enough to send many of us running away from our trusty personal computers. Fear not, though, because VBA's mathematical and financial keywords make these types of messy calculations easy — well, sort of.

VBA's mathematical keywords allow you to do amazing mathematical wonders such as calculating the square root or the natural logarithm of a number, or determining a number's absolute value.

Finances, schminances you say? Well, with VBA's financial functions, you can impress your tax accountant, or your real estate agent with amazing functions that calculate depreciation of assets using a variety of depreciation schedules. In addition, you'll be able to calculate both the interest and principal for any loan payment.

In this part . . .

- ✔ Calculating the sine of an angle
- ✔ Randomly picking numbers
- ✔ Calculating the natural logarithm of a number
- ✔ Amortizing an asset using a variety of depreciation methods
- ✔ Calculating the interest and principle portion of a loan payment
- ✔ Figuring the internal rate of return for a series of periodic cash flows

Operations Summary

Task	Keyword	Keyword Type
Calculate the absolute value of a number	Abs	Function
Calculate the arctangent of a number	Atn	Function
Calculate the cosine of an angle	Cos	Function
Calculate the depreciation of an asset using the double-declining balance or some other method	DDB	Function
Calculate the future value of an annuity	FV	Function
Calculate the interest payment for a period of an annuity	IPmt	Function
Calculate the interest rate for an annuity	Rate	Function
Calculate the internal rate of return for a series of periodic cash flows	IRR	Function
Calculate the modified internal rate of return for a series of periodic cash flows	MIRR	Function
Calculate the natural logarithm of a number	Log	Function
Calculate the net present value of an investment	NPV	Function
Calculate the number of periods for an annuity	NPer	Function
Calculate the payment for an annuity	Pmt	Function
Calculate the present value of an annuity	PV	Function
Calculate the principal payment for a period of an annuity	PPmt	Function
Calculate the result of "e" raised to a power	Exp	Function
Calculate the sign of a number	Sgn	Function
Calculate the sine of an angle	Sin	Function
Calculate the square root of a number	Sqr	Function
Calculate the straight-line depreciation of an asset for a single period	SLN	Function
Calculate the sum-of-year's digits depreciation of an asset	SYD	Function
Calculate the tangent of an angle	Tan	Function
Initialize the random number generator	Randomize	Statement
Return a pseudo-random floating point number between 0 and 1	Rnd	Function

Abs (Function)

Description: Returns the absolute value of a number.

Syntax:

```
Abs( number )
```

Argument	Description
number	A numeric expression.

Example:

```
intReturn = Abs(-23)  '= 23
intReturn = Abs(3.45) '= 3.45
```

Notes: The absolute value of a number is the number without its sign.

Atn (Function)

Description: Returns a Double containing the arctangent of a number.

Syntax:

```
Atn( number )
```

Argument	Description
number	A numeric expression of type Double that represents the ratio of two sides of a right triangle .

Example: This example calculates the arctangent of 0.5773 in radians and then converts the answer (which Atn returns in radians) to degrees:

```
dblRadians = Atn(0.5773) '= 0.523561072885415
dblDegrees = dblRadians * 180 / 3.14159 '= 29.99
```

Notes: Atn is a trigonometric function (remember high school geometry?) that takes the ratio of two sides of a right triangle and returns the angle in radians between those two sides. In case you were wondering, the Atn function calculates the reverse of the Tan function.

You can convert the less familiar radians to degrees by multiplying the number of radians by 180 and dividing by pi.

Cos (Function)

Description: Returns a `Double` containing the cosine of an angle.

Syntax:

`Cos( number )`

Argument	Description
number	A number of type `Double` representing an angle in radians.

Example: This example calculates the cosine of a 45 degree angle:

```
dblAngle = 45
dblReturn = Cos(dblAngle * 3.14159 / 180) '= 0.71
```

Notes: The cosine is a trigonometric function that returns the ratio of two sides of a right triangle. It takes as its input an angle expressed in radians and returns the ratio of the side adjacent to the angle divided by the length of the hypotenuse. The return value of `Cos` ranges between -1 and 1.

You can convert the more familiar degrees to radians by multiplying the number of degrees by pi and dividing by 180.

DDB (Function)

Description: Returns a `Double` containing the depreciation of an asset for a specified period using the double-declining balance or some other method.

Syntax:

`DDB( cost, salvage, life, period [, factor] )`

Argument	Description
cost	A number of type `Double` specifying the initial cost of an asset.
salvage	A number of type `Double` specifying the asset value at the end of its useful life.
life	A number of type `Double` specifying the length of an asset's useful life.
period	A number of type `Double` specifying the period for which the asset depreciation is to be calculated. `Period` and `life` must be specified using the same unit. Must range between 1 and `life`.

Argument	Description
factor	Optional. A Variant number specifying the rate at which the balance should decline. Defaults to 2 (for a double-declining balance). Factor can be a fractional number but must be greater than zero.

Example: This example calculates the depreciation for the first period for a $10,000 asset with a salvage cost of $2,000, depreciated using double-declining depreciation over 60 one-month periods:

```
dblDep = DDB(10000, 2000, 5*12, 1)   '= 333.33
```

Notes: The double-declining balance depreciation method calculates depreciation at an accelerated rate, meaning that depreciation is higher in the earlier periods. For straight-line depreciation, use the SLN function instead. (***See also*** the SLN function later in this part.)

Exp (Function)

Description: Raises "e" to a power.

Syntax:

```
Exp( number )
```

Argument	Description
number	A number of type Double not to exceed 709.78712893.

Example: This code calculates "e" raised to the 5th power:

```
dblResult = Exp(5) '= 148.413159102577
```

Notes: The Exp function raises "e" (a special mathematical number of approximately 2.718282) to the specified power. Exp reverses the action of the Log function so that:

```
Log(Exp(number)) = number
```

FV (Function)

Description: Calculates the future value of an annuity based on periodic, fixed payments and a fixed interest rate.

Syntax:

```
FV( rate, nper, pmt [, pv] [, type] )
```

Argument	Description
rate	A Double number specifying the interest rate per period. If the interest rate is expressed annually, and payments are made monthly, you need to divide the rate by 12.
nper	An Integer specifying the total number of payment periods for the annuity.
pmt	A Double number specifying the amount of each payment.
pv	Optional. A Double number specifying the present worth of a series of future payments. Defaults to 0.
type	Optional. An Integer equal to 0 if payments are due at the end of the payment period, or 1 if payments are due at the beginning of the payment period. Defaults to 0.

Example: This example calculates the future value of a 10-year annuity with monthly contributions of $500 and a fixed interest rate of 5.5 percent:

```
dblValue = FV(.055/12, 12*10, -500) '= 79753.79
```

Notes: If pmt is negative, FV calculates the future value of an annuity; if pmt is positive, FV calculates the future value of payments for a loan.

Rate and nper must be specified using the same period units.

IPmt (Function)

Description: Calculates the interest payment for a given period of an annuity based on periodic, fixed payments and a fixed interest rate.

Syntax:

```
IPmt( rate, per, nper, pv [, fv] [, type] )
```

Argument	Description
rate	A Double number specifying the interest rate per period. If the interest rate is expressed annually, and payments are made monthly, you need to divide the rate by 12.
per	An Integer specifying the period for which to calculate the interest payment. Must be between 1 and nper.
nper	An Integer specifying the total number of payment periods for the annuity.
pv	A Double number specifying the present worth of a series of future payments. For a loan, this is the loan amount.

Argument	Description
fv	Optional. A Double number specifying the future value or cash balance you want after you've made the final payment. If you wish to save $200,000 for retirement, then fv should be 200000. The future value of a loan is $0.
type	Optional. An Integer equal to 0 if payments are due at the end of the payment period, or 1 if payments are due at the beginning of the payment period. Defaults to 0.

Example: This example calculates the interest portion of a 30-year mortgage payment for the first payment of a $200,000 loan at a 7.5 percent annual fixed interest rate:

```
dblInt1 = IPmt(.075/12, 1, 12*30, 200000)'= -1250
```

Notes: A negative return value indicates cash payments, a positive return value indicates dividends received.

Rate, per, and nper must be specified using the same period units.

IRR (Function)

Description: Calculates the internal rate of return for a series of periodic cash flows.

Syntax:

```
IRR( values( ) [, guess] )
```

Argument	Description
values()	An array of type Double specifying cash flow values. The array must contain at least one negative value (a payment) and one positive value (a receipt).
guess	Optional. A Double number specifying a value you estimate will be returned by IRR. Defaults to 0.1 (10 percent).

Example: This example calculates the internal rate of return for a series of six payments and receipts:

```
Dim dblCashFlow(1 To 6) As Double
Dim dblIRR As Double

dblCashFlow(1) = -22000
dblCashFlow(2) = 5500
dblCashFlow(3) = -100
dblCashFlow(4) = 3400
dblCashFlow(5) = -450
dblCashFlow(6) = 340

dblIRR = IRR(dblCashFlow(), -0.5) '= -0.36
```

Notes: The internal rate of return is the interest rate received for an investment consisting of payments and receipts that occur at regular intervals.

The order of the values is important; this indicates to IRR the order in which the cash flows occurred. IRR calculates using multiple iterations. IRR stops iterating when the result is accurate to within 0.00001 percent. If IRR can't calculate a result within 20 iterations, it fails with a run-time error of 5 — Invalid procedure call or argument.

Log (Function)

Description: Returns a Double containing the natural logarithm of a number.

Syntax:

Log(*number*)

Argument	Description
number	A positive number of type Double.

Example:

This example calculates the natural log of 15:

dblLog = Log(15) '= 2.70805020110221

Notes: The natural logarithm is the log of a number to base "e." (e is a special mathematical number of approximately 2.718282.) Log reverses the action of the Exp function so that:

Log(Exp(*number*)) = *number*

MIRR (Function)

Description: Calculates the modified internal rate of return for a series of periodic cash flows.

Syntax:

MIRR(*values( )*, *finance_rate*, *reinvest_rate*)

Argument	Description
values( )	An array of type Double specifying cash flow values. The array must contain at least one negative value (a payment) and one positive value (a receipt).

Argument	Description
finance_rate	A number of type Double specifying the interest rate paid as the cost of financing.
reinvest_rate	A number of type Double specifying the interest rate received on gains from cash reinvestment.

Example: This example calculates the modified internal rate of return for a series of six payments and receipts with a finance rate of 8.5 percent and a reinvestment rate of 4.0 percent:

```
Dim dblCashFlow(1 To 6) As Double
Dim dblMIRR As Double

dblCashFlow(1) = -22000
dblCashFlow(2) = 5500
dblCashFlow(3) = -100
dblCashFlow(4) = 3400
dblCashFlow(5) = -450
dblCashFlow(6) = 340

dblMIRR = MIRR(dblCashFlow(), 0.85, 0.4) '= 0.0498
```

Notes: The modified internal rate of return is the internal rate of return when payments and receipts are financed at differing interest rates. (The internal rate of return is the interest rate received for an investment consisting of payments and receipts that occur at regular intervals.) The finance rate is the rate you pay for financing; the reinvest rate is the rate you receive on investments. (***See also*** IRR in this part.)

The order of the values is important; this indicates to MIRR the order in which the cash flows occurred.

NPer (Function)

Description: Calculates the number of periods for an annuity based on periodic, fixed payments and a fixed interest rate.

Syntax:

Nper(*rate, pmt, pv* [, *fv*] [, *type*] **)**

Argument	Description
rate	A Double number specifying the interest rate per period. If the interest rate is expressed annually, and payments are made monthly, you need to divide the rate by 12.
pmt	A Double number specifying the total payment (including both interest and principal) to be made each period.

(continued)

Argument	Description
pv	A Double number specifying the present worth of a series of future payments. For a loan, this is the loan amount.
fv	Optional. A Double number specifying the future value or cash balance you want after you've made the final payment. If you wish to save $200,000 for retirement, then fv should be 200000. The future value of a loan is $0.
type	Optional. An Integer number equal to 0 if payments are due at the end of the payment period, or 1 if payments are due at the beginning of the payment period. Defaults to 0.

Example: This example calculates the number of payments needed for a fixed-rate loan of $150,000 at an interest rate of 7.5 percent:

```
NPer(.075/12, -1000, 150000)    '= 444.999
```
This example calculates the number of contributions needed to a 6.0 percent fixed-rate annuity to achieve a future value of $200,000:

```
NPer(.06/12, -500, 0, 200000)    '= 220.271
```

Notes: For all arguments, cash paid out (for example, loan or annuity payments) are expressed as negative values, cash received (for example, dividend payments) are expressed as positive values.

NPV (Function)

Description: Calculates the net present value of an investment based on periodic, fixed payments and a fixed interest rate.

Syntax:

```
NPV( rate, values( ) )
```

Argument	Description
rate	A number of type Double specifying the discount rate over the length of the period.
values( )	An array of type Double specifying cash flow values. The array must contain at least one negative value (a payment) and one positive value (a receipt).

Example: This example calculates the net present value for a series of six payments and receipts with a discount rate of 1.5 percent:

```
Dim dblCashFlow(1 To 6) As Double
Dim dblNPV As Double
```

```
dblCashFlow(1) = -22000
dblCashFlow(2) = 5500
dblCashFlow(3) = -100
dblCashFlow(4) = 3400
dblCashFlow(5) = -450
dblCashFlow(6) = 340

dblNPV = NPV(0.015, dblCashFlow()) '= -13335.22
```

Notes: The net present value of an investment is the current value of a series of future payments and receipts.

The order of the values is important; this indicates to NPV the order in which the cash flows occurred.

The NPV investment begins one period before the first cash flow and ends with the last cash flow. If your first cash flow occurs at the beginning of the first period, you must add it to the return value of NPV, but not include it in the values array.

The related function, PV, calculates present value but unlike NPV requires cash flows to be fixed throughout the investment. PV also allows cash flows to begin at the end or the beginning of a period. (***See also*** PV in this part.)

Pmt (Function)

Description: Calculates the total payment (principal plus interest) for each period of an annuity based on periodic, fixed payments and a fixed interest rate.

Syntax:

```
Pmt( rate, nper, pv [, fv] [, type] )
```

See the description of arguments under the IPmt function.

Example: This example calculates a 30-year mortgage payment for a $200,000 loan at a 7.5 percent annual fixed interest rate:

```
dblPay = Pmt(.075/12, 12*30, 200000) '= -1398.43
```

Notes: A negative return value indicates cash payments, a positive return value indicates dividends received.

Rate and nper must be specified using the same period units.

The return value of IPmt added to PPmt for a given period should equal Pmt.

PPmt (Function)

Description: Calculates the principal payment for a given period of an annuity based on periodic, fixed payments and a fixed interest rate.

Syntax:

```
PPmt( rate, per, nper, pv [, fv] [, type] )
```

See the description of arguments under the PPmt function.

Example: This example calculates the principal portion of a 30-year mortgage payment for the first payment of a $200,000 loan at a 7.5 percent annual fixed interest rate (the answer is 148.43):

```
dblPri1 = PPmt(.075/12, 1, 12*30, 200000)
```

Notes: A negative return value indicates cash payments, a positive return value indicates dividends received.

Rate, per, and nper must be specified using the same period units.

The return value of IPmt added to PPmt for a given period should equal Pmt.

PV (Function)

Description: Calculates the present value of an annuity based on periodic, fixed payments to be paid in the future and a fixed interest rate.

Syntax:

```
PV( rate, nper, pmt [, fv] [, type] )
```

Argument	Description
rate	A Double number specifying the interest rate per period. If the interest rate is expressed annually, and payments are made monthly, you need to divide the rate by 12.
nper	An Integer specifying the total number of payment periods for the annuity.
pmt	A Double number specifying the amount of each payment.
fv	Optional. A Double number specifying the future value or cash balance you want after you've made the final payment. If you wish to save $200,000 for retirement, then fv should be 200000. The future value of a loan is $0.
type	Optional. An Integer number equal to 0 if payments are due at the end of the payment period, or 1 if payments are due at the beginning of the payment period. Defaults to 0.

Example: This example calculates the future value of a 30-year $200,000 loan at a 7.5 percent annual fixed interest rate and with $1,000 monthly payments:

```
dblFV = FV(.075/12, 12*30, -1000, 0) '= 1347445.42
```

Notes: A negative return value indicates cash payments, a positive return value indicates dividends received.

Rate and nper must be specified using the same period units.

Randomize (Statement)

Description: Initializes the random number generator.

Syntax:

```
Randomize [number]
```

Argument	Description
number	Optional. A number of type Variant that becomes the seed value for the random number generator. Defaults to use the system timer as the seed.

Example: This example illustrates the effect of using Randomize with two functions, one that uses Randomize and one that doesn't.

To see the effect, you must run the first function, FiveRandom1, repeatedly, resetting the VBA environment between each execution. This produces the same five random numbers every time FiveRandom1 runs.

```
Sub FiveRandom1()
    Dim intI As Integer
    For intI = 1 To 5
        Debug.Print intI, Rnd
    Next intI
End Sub
```

Now do the same with FiveRandom2 which is identical except for the inclusion of the Randomize statement. The sequence of numbers won't be the same:

```
Sub FiveRandom2()
    Dim intI As Integer
    Randomize
    For intI = 1 To 5
        Debug.Print intI, Rnd
    Next intI
End Sub
```

Notes: The random number generator built into VBA returns random numbers between 0 and 1 when you use the Rnd function. In actuality, Rnd, like other computer-based random number generators, generates pseudo-random numbers by making mathematical manipulations of very large numbers. Because of this, Rnd returns numbers from a fixed series of values. If you don't use the Randomize statement, prior to selecting a series of random numbers using Rnd, the sequence of numbers will always be the same!

The Randomize statement allows you pass a seed value to the random number generator that repositions it within its sequence of values. The result is that if you use Randomize before your first use of Rnd (since performing a reset of the VBA environment) with a seed value that is unique, the values returned by Rnd are different every time.

Using a unique seed value with Randomize is important If you use Randomize with the same seed value at the beginning of your procedure, you've gained nothing, because Randomize always repositions itself to the same place in the random number generator's fixed series of values. Thus, it's almost always best to call Randomize without a parameter, which tells VBA to use the system clock (which passes the number of seconds since midnight) as the seed value. It's very unlikely you will execute the Randomize statement at the very same time of day (to the hundredth of a second) twice.

Randomize does not effect whether Rnd sometimes selects duplicate numbers; this happens regardless of the use of Randomize.

Rate (Function)

Description: Calculates the interest rate for an annuity.

Syntax:

Rate(*nper, pmt, pv* [, *fv*] [, *type*] [, *guess*] **)**

Argument	Description
nper	An Integer specifying the total number of payment periods for the annuity.
pmt	A Double number specifying the total amount of each payment which should include both principal and interest.
pv	A Double number specifying the present worth of a series of future payments. For a loan, this is the loan amount.

Argument	Description
fv	Optional. A Double number specifying the future value or cash balance you want after you've made the final payment. If you wish to save $200,000 for retirement, then fv should be 200000. The future value of a loan is $0.
type	Optional. An Integer number equal to 0 if payments are due at the end of the payment period, or 1 if payments are due at the beginning of the payment period. Defaults to 0.
guess	Optional. A Double number specifying a value you estimate will be returned by Rate. Defaults to 0.1 (10 percent).

Example: This example calculates the annual interest rate of a 30-year fixed-rate mortgage for $200,000 and with a $1398.43 total monthly payment (the answer is 0.075):

```
dblAnnRate = Rate(12*30, -1398.43, 200000) * 12
```

Notes: For all arguments, cash paid out (for example, loan or annuity payments) are expressed as negative values, cash received (for example, dividend payments) are expressed as positive values.

Rate calculates using iterations. Rate stops iterating when the result is accurate to within 0.00001 percent. If Rate can't calculate a result within 20 iterations, it fails with a runtime error of 5 — Invalid procedure call or argument.

Rate returns the interest rate as a decimal value; if you want a percentage you must multiply the result by 100. Thus, in the example, 0.075 is the same as 7.5 percent.

Rnd (Function)

Description: Returns a Single containing a pseudo-random floating point number between 0 and 1.

Syntax:

```
Rnd [( number )]
```

Argument	Description
number	Optional. A number of type Single that affects how random numbers are selected. Number can be one of the following values:

Number value	Rnd *returns*
< 0	The same number every time using number as the seed.

(continued)

Number value	Rnd **returns**
0	The most recently-generated random number.
> 0	The next random number in the sequence. Rnd also returns the next random number in the sequence if number is omitted.

Example: This subroutine generates ten random whole numbers between a lower and upper bound and prints them to the Immediate window:

```
Sub RndIntegers(intLower As Integer, _
  intUpper As Integer)
    Dim intI As Integer
    Dim intRnd As Integer
    Randomize
    For intI = 1 To 10
        ' this is how you select whole numbers
        ' between a lower and upper bound
        intRnd = Int((intUpper - intLower + 1) _
        * Rnd() + intLower)
        Debug.Print intI, intRnd
    Next intI
End Sub
```

Notes: Because Rnd always returns values between 0 and 1, you need to transform the returned values to get randomly selected whole numbers. The formula is:

```
Int((Upper - Lower + 1) * Rnd() + Lower)
```

The Rnd function selects pseudo-random numbers from a fixed series of values. In order to generate a different set of numbers each time, you should use the Randomize statement at the beginning of the procedure. ***See also*** the discussion of the Randomize statement earlier in this part for more information.

Sgn (Function)

Description: Returns the sign of a number.

Syntax:

Sgn(*number*)

Argument	Description
number	A number of type Double.

Sgn returns a Variant of the Integer subtype as follows:

Number	Sgn *returns*
< 0	-1
0	0
> 0	1

Example:

```
intSign1 = Sgn(1.34)   '= 1
intSign2 = Sgn(-45)    '= -1
intSign3 = Sgn(0)      '= 0
```

Notes: The Abs function returns the number without its sign.

Sin (Function)

Description: Returns a Double containing the sine of an angle.

Syntax:

```
Sin( number )
```

Argument	Description
number	A number of type Double representing an angle in radians.

Example: This example calculates the sine of a 45 degree angle:

```
dblAngle = 45
dblReturn = Sin(dblAngle * 3.14159 / 180)  '= 0.71
```

Notes: The sine is a trigonometric function that returns the ratio of two sides of a right triangle. The sine function takes as its input an angle expressed in radians and returns the ratio of the side opposite to the angle divided by the length of the hypotenuse. The return value of Sin ranges between -1 and 1.

You can convert the more familiar degrees to radians by multiplying the number of degrees by pi and dividing by 180.

SLN (Function)

Description: Returns a Double containing the straight-line depreciation of an asset.

Syntax:

```
SLN( cost, salvage, life )
```

Argument	Description
cost	A number of type Double specifying the initial cost of an asset.
salvage	A number of type Double specifying the asset value at the end of its useful life.
life	A number of type Double specifying the length of an asset's useful life.

Example: This example calculates the straight-line depreciation of a $10,000 asset with a salvage value of $2,000 over 60 one-month periods:

```
dblDep = SLN(10000, 2000, 5*12)   '= 133.33
```

Sqr (Function)

Description: Returns a Double containing the square root of a number.

Syntax:

```
Sqr( number )
```

Argument	Description
number	A number of type Double.

Example:

```
dblRoot = Sqr(9) '= 3
dblRoot = Sqr(5) '= 2.23606797749979
```

SYD (Function)

Description: Returns a Double containing the depreciation of an asset for a specified period using the sum-of-years' digits depreciation method.

Syntax:

```
SYD( cost, salvage, life, period )
```

Argument	Description
cost	A number of type Double specifying the initial cost of an asset.
salvage	A number of type Double specifying the asset value at the end of its useful life.

Argument	Description
life	A number of type Double specifying the length of an asset's useful life.
period	A number of type Double specifying the period for which the asset depreciation is to be calculated. Period and life must be specified using the same unit. Must range between 1 and life.

Example: This example calculates the depreciation for the first period for a $10,000 asset with a salvage value of $2,000, depreciated using sum-of-years' digits depreciation over 60 one-month periods:

```
dblDep = SYD(10000, 2000, 5*12, 1)   '= 262.30
```

Tan (Function)

Description: Returns a Double containing the tangent of an angle.

Syntax:

```
Tan( number )
```

Argument	Description
number	A number of type Double representing an angle in radians.

Example:

This example calculates the tangent of a 45 degree angle:

```
dblAngle = 45
dblReturn = Tan(dblAngle * 3.14159 / 180) '= 0.99
```

Notes: The tangent is a trigonometric function that returns the ratio of two sides of a right triangle. The tangent function takes as its input an angle expressed in radians and returns the ratio of the side opposite to the angle divided by the length of the side adjacent to the angle.

You can convert the more familiar degrees to radians by multiplying the number of degrees by pi and dividing by 180.

Part X

Miscellaneous

Not every VBA keyword fits neatly into a category. So I stuck all those keywords in this, the miscellaneous part. Here you find statements and functions you can use to create compiler directives, convert color codes, create MsgBox and InputBox dialog boxes, sound a tone, read and write values to the registry, send keystrokes to the keyboard buffer, and document your programs.

In this part . . .

✔ **Sounding a tone using the PC speaker**

✔ **Reading and writing values to the registry**

✔ **Deleting keys from the registry**

✔ **Converting color codes**

✔ **Creating MsgBox dialog**

✔ **Documenting your VBA code**

✔ **Sending keystrokes to the keyboard buffer**

Keyword Summary

Task	Keyword	Keyword Type
Convert a QuickBasic-style color number into an RGB color value	QBColor	Function
Convert RGB component values into an RGB color value	RGB	Function
Declare a compiler constant	#Const	Directive
Delete a key or section from a VBA application node in the registry	DeleteSetting	Statement
Direct the compiler to compile a selected block of code	#If...Then ...#Else	Directive
Display a message box dialog	MsgBox	Statement
Display a message box dialog and return a value that indicates which button was pressed	MsgBox	Function
Display a simple dialog box to capture user input	InputBox	Function
Document your VBA code using a comment	Rem	Statement
Get an operating system environment variable	Environ	Function
Get the command line argument used to start the VBA host application	Command	Function
Retrieve a list of keys from a VBA application node in the registry	GetAll Settings	Function
Retrieve the value of a single key from a VBA application node in the registry	GetSetting	Function
Save a value to a key in a VBA application node in the registry	SaveSetting	Statement
Send keystrokes to the active window as if they were typed using the keyboard	SendKeys	Statement
Sound a tone using the PC speaker	Beep	Statement
Yield to the operating system so it can process other operations	DoEvents	Function

#Const (Directive)

Description: Declares a compiler constant.

Syntax:

```
#Const constname = expression
```

Argument	Description
constname	Name of the constant.
expression	A literal string, number, or numeric expression.

Example: This example illustrates how you can use constant directives to help debug your procedures during development. ReverseIt2 includes debug code that prints out the contents of strString and strReverse to the Debug window for each cycle of the loop but only if conDebug is set to True.

Place this constant directive in the declarations section of a module:

```
#Const conDebug = True
```

Here's the ReverseIt2 function:

```
Function ReverseIt2(ByVal strStr As String) As
    String
    Dim strReverse As String
    Do While Len(strStr) > 0
        strReverse = strReverse + Right(strStr, 1)
        strStr = Left(strStr, Len(strStr) - 1)
        #If conDebug Then
            Debug.Print "strStr=" & strStr & _
            ", " & "strReverse=" & strReverse
        #End If
    Loop
    ReverseIt2 = strReverse
End Function
```

Notes: You may declare compiler constants within a procedure or within a module's declarations section, but the constant is always evaluated at the module level.

You may create a project-global compiler constant by using the Conditional Compilation Arguments text box of the General tab of the *project_name* Properties dialog box (choose Tools⇨*project_name* Properties). (In Microsoft Access, you must use the Advanced tab of the Options dialog box.) Constants defined here are global for the project but can only be of the Integer data type.

If you declare the same compiler constant using both the #Const compiler directive and the *project_name* Properties dialog box, the #Const compiler directive takes precedence.

#If...Then...#Else (Directive)

Description: Conditionally compiles a block of code based on the current value of a compiler constant.

Syntax:

```
#If condition Then
    [statements]
[#Elseif condition-1 Then
    [elseifstatements]]
    ...
[#Elseif condition-n Then
    [elseifstatements]]
[#Else
    [elsestatements]]
#End If
```

Argument	Description
condition	An expression that evaluates to True or False. If the expression is Null, the expression is treated as if it's False.
statements	Optional. One or more statements to compile into the project if condition is True.
elseifstatements	Optional. One or more statements to compile into the project if the associated condition-n is True.
elsestatements	Optional. One of more statements to compile into the project if no other condition is True.

Example: See the example under the #Const directive keyword.

Notes: The behavior of the #If...Then...#Else directive is identical to that of the If...Then...Else statement except that instead of conditionally executing code, the #If...Then...#Else directive conditionally compiles code into the VBA project.

Beep (Statement)

Description: Sounds a tone using the PC speaker.

Syntax:

```
Beep
```

Example:

```
Beep
```

Notes: The frequency and duration of the tone varies from computer to computer.

Command (Function)

Description: Returns a `String` containing the cmd command line argument used to start the VBA host application.

Syntax:

```
Command( )
```

Example:

```
strCmdLine = Command()
```

Notes: Command returns the portion of the command line following `"/cmd"` which must occur at the end of the command line after all other arguments.

DeleteSetting (Statement)

Description: Deletes a key or section from a VBA application node in the registry.

Syntax:

```
DeleteSetting appname, section [, key]
```

Argument	Description
appname	A `String` specifying an application or project section of the HKEY_CURRENT_USER\Software\VB and VBA Program Settings node of the registry.
section	A `String` specifying a section of the HKEY_CURRENT_USER\Software\VB and VBA Program Settings*appname* node of the registry.
key	Optional. A `String` specifying a key under the HKEY_CURRENT_USER\Software\VB and VBA Program Settings*appname**section* node of the registry. If omitted, `DeleteSetting` deletes the entire section.

Example: This example removes the `DeleteSetting` key from the VBA for Dummies Quick Reference\Miscellaneous section of the VBA application node in the registry:

```
DeleteSetting "VBA for Dummies Quick Reference", _
  "Miscellaneous", "DeleteSetting"
```

This example removes the entire Miscellaneous section from the VBA for Dummies Quick Reference section of the VBA application node in the registry:

```
DeleteSetting "VBA for Dummies Quick Reference", _
"Miscellaneous"
```

Notes: If you attempt to use `DeleteSetting` to delete a key that doesn't exist, VBA generates a runtime error.

DoEvents (Function)

Description: Yields to the operating system so it can process other operations.

Syntax:

```
DoEvents
```

Example: This example closes an Automation connection to Word but gives Word some processor time so it can carry out the `Quit` command prior to destroying the mobjWOrd object:

```
mobjWord.Quit
DoEvents
Set mobjWord = Nothing
```

Notes: `DoEvents` is useful whenever you need to give some other process more processor time. When executed, `DoEvents` passes control to the operating system, which allows it to process pending events in its queue as well as to process keys in the `SendKeys` queue.

Environ (Function)

Description: Returns a `String` containing an operating system environment variable.

Syntax:

```
Environ ( expression )
```

Argument	Description
expression	Can be a string, specifying the name of an existing operating system environment parameter, or a number specifying the ordinal number of an environment parameter.

Example: This example assumes that the prompt setting for this machine is set to pg, and that path is the second environment parameter:

```
strPath = Environ("prompt")    '= "$p$g"
strPrm2 = Environ(2)           '= "PROMPT=$p$g"
```

Notes: When you pass Environ a string argument, Environ returns the value of the matching environment parameter. When you pass Environ a numeric argument, however, Environ returns the name of the environment parameter followed by an equal sign operator and the value of the parameter.

GetAllSettings (Function)

Description: Returns a Variant which contains an array of keys from a VBA application node in the registry.

Syntax:

GetAllSettings (*appname, section*)

Argument	Description
appname	A String specifying an application or project section of HKEY_CURRENT_USER\Software\VB and VBA Program Settings node of the registry.
section	A String specifying a section of the HKEY_CURRENT_USER\Software\VB and VBA Program Settings*appname* node of the registry.

Example: This example prints to the debug window all of the settings under the VBA for Dummies Quick Reference\Publishing node of the VBA application node in the registry:

```
Dim varKeys As Variant
Dim intI As Integer

varKeys = GetAllSettings( _
 "VBA for Dummies Quick Reference", _
 "Publishing")

For intI = LBound(varKeys, 1) To UBound(varKeys, 1)
   Debug.Print varKeys(intI, 0) & _
     "=" & varKeys(intI, 1)
Next intI
```

Notes: Use the GetSetting function to retrieve the value of a single key.

GetSetting (Function)

Description: Returns a String containing the value of a key from a VBA application node in the registry.

Syntax:

GetSetting (*appname, section, key* [, *default*])

Argument	Description
appname	A String specifying an application or project section of the HKEY_CURRENT_USER\Software\VB and VBA Program Settings node of the system registry.
section	A String specifying a section of the HKEY_CURRENT_USER\Software\VB and VBA Program Settings*appname* node of the registry.
key	A String specifying a key under the HKEY_CURRENT_USER\Software\VB and VBA Program Settings*appname**section* node of the registry.
default	Optional. A String to return if no value is set in the key or if the key doesn't exist. Defaults to a zero-length string.

Example: This example returns the String matching the requested key or "(not published)" if the key doesn't exist or was never set to a value:

```
strKey = GetSetting( _
"VBA for Dummies Quick Reference", _
"Publishing", "Year", "(not published)")
```

Notes: Use the GetAllSettings function to retrieve the names and values for a entire section.

InputBox (Function)

Description: Displays a simple dialog box to capture user input and waits for the user to click on the OK or Cancel button.

Syntax:

InputBox (*prompt* [, *title*] [, *default*] [, *xpos*]
      [, *ypos*] [, *helpfile, context*])

Argument	Description
prompt	String expression that displays in the dialog box to prompt the user for input. Can be up to approximately 1,024 characters long.
title	Optional. String expression to display in the title bar of the dialog box. If omitted, the host application name is used.
default	Optional. String expression displayed in the text box of the dialog box. If omitted, the text box contains a zero-length string.

Argument	Description
xpos	Optional. A numeric expression that specifies (in twips) the horizontal screen position at which to display the dialog box. If omitted, or if specified, but ypos is omitted, the dialog box appears centered on the screen.
ypos	Optional. A numeric expression that specifies (in twips) the vertical screen position at which to display the dialog box. If omitted, or if specified, but xpos is omitted, the dialog box appears centered on the screen.
helpfile	Optional. The name of a helpfile to link to the dialog box. If specified, a third button, labeled Help, is added to the dialog box. If specified, context must also be specified. If omitted, no help file is associated with the dialog box.
context	Optional. A context ID of helpfile to link to the dialog box. If specified, a third button, labeled Help, is added to the dialog box. If specified, helpfile must also be specified. If omitted, no help file is associated with the dialog box.

Example: This example requests the user's favorite color and stores the answer in strColor:

```
strColor = InputBox("Your favorite color?", _
  "The Third Question", "red, no blue")
```

Notes: If the user dismisses the dialog box by clicking on the Cancel button, a zero-length string is returned, regardless of whether a default was specified.

The dialog box created by InputBox is quite rudimentary. In most cases, you should use a user form (or an Access form if you're using Microsoft Access) to produce a more user-friendly interface for your application.

MsgBox (Function)

Description: Displays a message box dialog box and returns a Long that indicates which button was pressed.

Syntax:

```
MsgBox ( prompt [, buttons] [, title] [, helpfile,
  context] )
```

Argument	Description
prompt	String expression that displays in the dialog box to prompt the user for input. Can be up to approximately 1,024 characters long.
buttons	Optional. An Integer value whose sum indicates which buttons to display (0-5); the icon, if any, to display (16-64); the default button (0, or 256-768); and whether the dialog box

Argument	Description
	should be application or system modal (0 or 4096). If omitted, the dialog box contains a single OK button, no icon, the OK button is the default button, and the dialog box is application modal. The values to choose from are as follows:

Constant	Value	Meaning
vbOKOnly	0	Displays OK button only
vbOKCancel	1	Displays OK and Cancel buttons
vbAbortRetryIgnore	2	Displays Abort, Retry, and Ignore buttons
vbYesNoCancel	3	Displays Yes, No, and Cancel buttons
vbYesNo	4	Displays Yes and No buttons
vbRetryCancel	5	Displays Retry and Cancel buttons
vbCritical	16	Displays Critical Message icon
vbQuestion	32	Displays Warning Query icon
vbExclamation	48	Displays Warning Message icon
vbInformation	64	Displays Information Message icon
vbDefaultButton1	0	First button is default
vbDefaultButton2	256	Second button is default
vbDefaultButton3	512	Third button is default
vbDefaultButton4	768	Fourth (help) button is default
vbApplicationModal	0	Application modal; you must respond to the message box before continuing work in the current application
vbSystemModal	4096	System modal; all applications are suspended until you respond to the message box

Argument	Description
title	Optional. `String` expression to display in the title bar of the dialog box. If omitted, the host application name is used.
helpfile	Optional. The name of a helpfile to link to the dialog box. If specified, a third button, labeled Help, is added to the dialog box. If specified, `context` must also be specified. If omitted, no help file is associated with the dialog box.
context	Optional. A context ID of `helpfile` to link to the dialog box. If specified, a third button, labeled Help, is added to the dialog box. If specified, `helpfile` must also be specified. If omitted, no help file is associated with the dialog box.

The return value of `MsgBox` may be one of the following values, which indicates the button that was pressed to dismiss the dialog box:

Constant	Value	Meaning
vbOK	1	OK button pressed
vbCancel	2	Cancel button pressed
vbAbort	3	Abort button pressed
vbRetry	4	Retry button pressed
vbIgnore	5	Ignore button pressed
vbYes	6	Yes button pressed
vbNo	7	No button pressed

Example: This example displays a message box dialog, sticking the return value in intResp:

```
intResp = MsgBox("Do you wish to continue?", _
  vbYesNo + vbQuestion + vbDefaultButton2, _
  "It's getting late...")
```

Notes: If the `MsgBox` includes a Cancel button, then pressing the Escape key has the same effect as clicking on the Cancel button.

There's also a statement version of `MsgBox` that's useful if you display only a single button and thus don't care about any return value. (***See also*** `MsgBox` statement in this part.)

MsgBox (Statement)

Description: Displays a message box dialog box.

Syntax:

```
MsgBox prompt [, buttons] [, title] [, helpfile,
    context]
```

Argument	Description
prompt	String expression that displays in the dialog box to prompt the user for input. Can be up to approximately 1,024 characters long.
buttons	Optional. An Integer value whose sum indicates which buttons to display (0-5); the icon, if any, to display (16-64); the default button (0, or 256-768); and whether the dialog should be application or system modal (0 or 4096). If omitted, and the dialog box contains a single OK button, no icon, the OK button is the default button, and the dialog box is application modal. (**See also** MsgBox function for a list of constants and their meanings.)
title	Optional. String expression to display in the title bar of the dialog box. If omitted, the host application name is used.
helpfile	Optional. The name of a helpfile to link to the dialog box. If specified, a third button, and labeled Help, is added to the dialog box. If specified, context must also be specified. If omitted, no help file is associated with the dialog box.
context	Optional. A context ID of helpfile to link to the dialog box. If specified, a third button, labeled Help, is added to the dialog box. If specified, helpfile must also be specified. If omitted, no help file is associated with the dialog box.

Example: This example displays a message box dialog using the MsgBox statement. Because there's only one button, there's no need to capture a return value:

```
Call MsgBox("Fatal error. Cannot continue.", _
    vbOKOnly + vbCritical, "Fatal Error")
```

Notes: If you need to display more than one button, use the MsgBox function, not the MsgBox statement so you can detect which button the user pressed.

QBColor (Function)

Description: Converts a QuickBasic-style color number into an RGB color value.

Syntax:

```
QBColor ( color )
```

Argument	Description
color	A whole number between 0 and 15 indicating a color code used in earlier versions of Basic (including Quick Basic and Visual Basic for MS-DOS). The possible values of the color argument are as follows:

Value	Color	Value	Color
0	Black	8	Gray
1	Blue	9	Light Blue
2	Green	10	Light Green
3	Cyan	11	Light Cyan
4	Red	12	Light Red
5	Magenta	13	Light Magenta
6	Yellow	14	Light Yellow
7	White	15	Bright White

Example: This example (if attached to a user form's Initialize event) sets the background color of the form to light magenta as the form loads:

```
Private Sub UserForm_Initialize()
    Me.BackColor = QBColor(13)
End Sub
```

Notes: You can also use the RGB function to return an RGB color value.

Rem (Statement)

Description: Documents your VBA code with a comment.

Syntax: There are two forms of the Rem statement:

```
Rem [comment]
```

and

```
'[comment]
```

Argument	Description
comment	Optional. A comment used to document the program.

Example: The following lines of code each contain a comment:

```
Rem an old-fashioned block-style style comment
'a more typical block-style comment
varReturn = MsgBox("What?") 'an in-line comment
```

Notes: The first version of the Rem statement is seldom used. Most VBA programmers prefer to use the apostrophe version of the Rem statement because it's easier to type and easier to read.

Comments provide an excellent mechanism for documenting your code. Use them generously throughout your code. It's better to comment on the why rather than how because the latter should be obvious from the actual code.

RGB (Function)

Description: Converts RGB component values into an RGB color value.

Syntax:

```
RGB ( red, green, blue )
```

Argument	Description
red	Number in the range 0-255, indicating the red component of the color.
green	Number in the range 0-255, indicating the green component of the color.
blue	Number in the range 0-255, indicating the blue component of the color.

Example: This example (if attached to a user form's Initialize event) sets the background color of the form to pure red as the form loads:

```
Private Sub UserForm_Initialize()
    Me.BackColor = RGB(255,0,0)
End Sub
```

Notes: Any argument exceeding 255 (while still an Integer) is treated as if it were 255. Floating-point arguments are rounded to the nearest whole number. Negative arguments and non-Integer arguments cause a run-time error.

SaveSetting (Statement)

Description: Saves a value to a key in a VBA application node in the registry.

Syntax:

```
SaveSetting appname, section, key, setting
```

Argument	Description
appname	A String specifying an application or project section of the HKEY_CURRENT_USER\Software\VB and VBA Program Settings node of the registry.
section	A String specifying a section of the HKEY_CURRENT_USER\Software\VB and VBA Program Settings*appname* node of the registry.
key	A String specifying a key under the HKEY_CURRENT_USER\Software\VB and VBA Program Settings*appname**section* node of the registry.
setting	A String to save to the key.

Example: This example saves the value "Dummies Press" to the Publisher key of the VBA for Dummies Quick Reference\Publishing section of the VBA application node in the registry:

```
SaveSetting "VBA for Dummies Quick Reference", _
  "Publishing", "Publisher", "Dummies Press"
```

Notes: A runtime error occurs if VBA cannot save a key to the registry.

On 16-bit Windows platforms, VBA uses an .INI file named *appname* instead of registry entries.

SendKeys (Statement)

Description: Sends keystrokes to the active window as if they were typed using the keyboard.

Syntax:

```
SendKeys string [, wait]
```

Argument	Description
string	String expression representing the sequence of keystrokes to send. For non-alphabetic characters, use one of the following codes :

Key	Code
BACKSPACE	{BACKSPACE}, {BS}, or {BKSP}
BREAK	{BREAK}
CAPS LOCK	{CAPSLOCK}
DEL or DELETE	{DELETE} or {DEL}
DOWN ARROW	{DOWN}

(continued)

END	{END}
ENTER	{ENTER} or ~
ESC	{ESC}
HELP	{HELP}
HOME	{HOME}
INS or INSERT	{INSERT} or {INS}
LEFT ARROW	{LEFT}
NUM LOCK	{NUMLOCK}
PAGE DOWN	{PGDN}
PAGE UP	{PGUP}
PRINT SCREEN	{PRTSC}
RIGHT ARROW	{RIGHT}
SCROLL LOCK	{SCROLLLOCK}
TAB	{TAB}
UP ARROW	{UP}
Fx function key	{Fx}
SHIFT	+
CTRL	^
ALT	%

wait	Optional. A Boolean value specifying whether VBA waits before sending the keystrokes. If False (the default), control is returned immediately after the keystrokes are sent. If True, the keystrokes must be processed before control is returned.

Example: This example uses SendKeys to type "hello world" followed by the Enter key without waiting for the keys to be processed:

```
SendKeys "hello world{Enter}"
```

Notes: If you need to specify a shifted keystroke or a keystroke to be pressed simultaneously with the Ctrl or Alt keys, precede the keystroke with the modifier key. For example, to send Ctrl+S, you need to use the following SendKeys statement:

```
SendKeys "^s"
```

Only use SendKeys when all other methods of solving a problem have failed. Code containing SendKeys statements often fails when converted to later versions of a product, or when used in an international setting.

Part XI

Procedures

The basic unit of code in VBA is the procedure. There are five types of procedures: functions, subroutines (often called *subs*), and three types of property procedures (get, let, and set). Functions and subs can go into any module, whereas property procedures can go only into class modules. There's also a pseudo-procedure statement you can use — the Declare statement — to tell VBA you'd like to call a procedure that exists outside of your project in an external dynamic link library (DLL).

In this part . . .

- ✔ **Calling subroutines**
- ✔ **Creating functions and subroutines**
- ✔ **Creating user-defined properties using property procedures**
- ✔ **Declaring external API procedures**

Keyword Summary

Task	Keyword	Keyword Type
Call a procedure	Call	Statement
Create a function	Function	Statement
Create a procedure in a class module that assigns the value of a property	Property Let	Statement
Create a procedure in a class module that returns the value of a property	Property Get	Statement
Create a procedure in a class module that sets a property to point to an object	Property Set	Statement
Create a subroutine	Sub	Statement
Declare a reference to an external procedure in a dynamic link library	Declare	Statement

Call (Statement)

Description: Calls a procedure.

Syntax: The two forms of the Call statement are

Call *name* [(*argumentlist*)]

and

name [*argumentlist*]

Argument	Description
name	Name of a procedure.
argumentlist	Optional. Arguments to the procedure that may be either positional or named parameters. If using the first form of the Call syntax to call a procedure with one or more parameters, you must include parentheses around the parameter list. If using the second form of the Call syntax (without the Call keyword), don't include the parentheses. If the procedure is located in an external DLL, the ByVal or ByRef keyword may precede each argument to force VBA to pass the argument to the DLL procedure by value or by reference, respectively.

Example: Here are three different ways to use the `Call` statement to call a subroutine named LookupName. The first two examples use positional arguments; the last example uses named arguments:

```
Call LookupName("Bill", "Gates")
LookupName "Bill", "Gates"
Call LookupName(strLastName:="Gates", _
   strFirstName:= "Bill")
```

Notes: To pass an array to a procedure, use the name of the array followed by an empty set of parentheses.

Prior versions of VBA did not let you execute functions with the `Call` statement. While you can now execute functions with the `Call` statement, you don't have access to the function's returned value. In general, you should execute functions by assigning their return value to a variable instead of using the `Call` statement.

Declare (Statement)

Description: Declares a reference to an external procedure located in a dynamic link library.

Syntax: The `Declare` statement has two forms. The first form is used with external subroutines:

```
[Public | Private] Declare Sub name Lib "libname"
   [Alias "aliasname"] [([arglist])]
```

The second form is used with external functions:

```
[Public | Private] Declare Function name Lib
   "libname" [Alias "aliasname"] [([arglist])] [As
   type]
```

Argument	Description
`Public	Private`	Optional. Use `Public` to indicate that the DLL procedure is available outside the current module or `Private` to indicate the DLL procedure can be called only from other procedures in the current module. Defaults to `Public`.
`name`	The case-sensitive name of the external procedure, or, if the alias keyword is used, the local name by which this procedure will be known.
`libname`	The name of the dynamic link library that contains the procedure.

Argument	Description
aliasname	Optional. If used, aliasname is the case-sensitive name of the procedure in the DLL and name becomes the local *alias* for the external procedure. If omitted, no alias is used and name must refer to the actual name of the procedure. You may also use an ordinal aliasname to indicate the procedure by its ordinal position in the DLL. In this case, you must precede the number with a pound sign (#).
arglist	Optional. The list and data type of arguments that must match the parameters the external procedure expects.
type	Optional. The data type of the return value. If omitted, the return value is typed as a Variant.

The arglist parameter must follow this syntax:

```
[Optional] [ByVal | ByRef] [ParamArray] varname[()]
    [As type]
```

Part	Description
Optional	Optional. Used to indicate that this argument is not required. Any arguments after the first optional argument must also be optional. Cannot be used with ParamArray arguments. If omitted, the argument is required.
ByVal	ByRef	Optional. Used to indicate that the parameter is passed by value or by reference, respectively. If omitted, defaults to ByRef.
ParamArray	Optional. Indicates the parameter is an optional array of Variant elements. Must be the last parameter in the list.
varname	Placeholder name of the parameter. The name you use here is arbitrary but must follow standard VBA naming conventions.
()	Optional. Indicates that varname is an array. If omitted, varname is a scalar (non-array) variable.
type	Optional. The data type of the variable. Defaults to Variant.

Example: Here's a Declare statement for a subroutine with one parameter and an alias:

```
Declare Sub pelOutputDebugStr Lib "winmm.dll"_ Alias
    "OutputDebugStr" (ByVal lpszOutputString_ As
        String)
```

Notes: Declare statements used in class and form modules must include the Private keyword; you cannot specify public declare statements in a class or form module. (In Microsoft Access, this is also true for report modules.)

Specifying each parameter, its data type, and the `ByVal`/`ByRef` keyword correctly and in the correct order is very important. An incorrectly specified parameter may crash your computer and you may lose all unsaved work. Therefore, before testing a new `Declare` statement, save everything!

Function (Statement)

Description: Creates a function in the current module.

Syntax:

```
[Public | Private] [Static] Function name
    [(arglist)]
[As type]
    [statements]
    [name = expression]
    [Exit Function]
    [statements]
    [name = expression]
End Function
```

Argument	Description
Public | Private	Optional. Use `Public` to indicate that the function is available outside the current module or `Private` to indicate the function can only be called from other procedures in the current module. (For class and form modules, the `Public` keyword causes VBA to make the function a method of the class.) Defaults to `Public`.
Static	Optional. Indicates that all variables declared inside the function are treated as static variables (their values are preserved between calls to the function). If omitted, all variables declared inside the function are treated non-statically.
name	The name of the function.
arglist	Optional. A list of arguments and their data types.
type	Optional. The data type of the return value. If omitted, the return value is typed as a `Variant`.
statements	Optional. One or more VBA statements.

(continued)

Argument	Description
expression	Optional. The return value of the function. If you do not include a "name = expression" statement, the return value defaults to the default value of the return value (which depends upon the data type of the return value).
Exit Function	Optional. Causes the function to be immediately exited.

The arglist parameter must follow this syntax:

```
[Optional] [ByVal | ByRef] [ParamArray] varname[()]
    [As type] [= defaultvalue]
```

Part	Description
Optional	Optional. Used to indicate that this argument is not required. Any arguments after the first optional argument must also be optional. Cannot be used with ParamArray arguments. If omitted, the argument is required.
ByVal | ByRef	Optional. Used to indicate that the parameter is passed by value or by reference, respectively. If omitted, defaults to ByRef. When a parameter is passed *by value*, changes made to the parameter within the function are *not* reflected back in the calling procedure because the changes are made to a local copy of the parameter. In contrast, when a parameter is passed *by reference*, any changes made to the parameter *are* reflected in the calling procedure.
ParamArray	Optional. Indicates the parameter is an optional array of Variant elements. Must be the last parameter in the list.
varname	Name of the parameter.
()	Optional. Indicates that varname is an array. If omitted, varname is a scalar (non-array) variable.
type	Optional. The data type of the variable. Defaults to Variant.
defaultvalue	Optional. For optional arguments, the default value to assign if the argument is omitted when calling the function. Can only be used with the Optional keyword. For Object variables, can only be Nothing.

Example: This trivial function has two Integer parameters and returns a Long:

```
Function AddEmUp(intLower As Integer, _
  intUpper As Integer) As Long
    Dim lngSum As Long
    Dim intCount As Integer
    lngSum = 0
    For intCount = intLower To intUpper
        lngSum = lngSum + intCount
    Next intCount
    AddEmUp = lngSum
End Function
```

Notes: You can call a function using either an assignment statement that assigns the return value to a variable or a `Call` statement. For example, the above function could be called using either of the following:

```
lngSum = AddEmUp(5, 6)
Call AddEmUp(5, 6)
```

If you use a `Call` statement, however, the return value is unavailable, which makes this method of calling a function useless unless you don't care about the function's return value.

In general, if your procedure doesn't have any need to return something to the calling procedure, you should use a subroutine instead of a function.

Property Get (Statement)

Description: Creates a procedure in a class module that returns the value of a property.

Syntax:

```
[Public | Private] [Static] Property Get name
    ([arglist]) [As type]
    [statements]
    [name = expression]
    [Exit Property]
    [statements]
    [name = expression]
End Function
```

Argument	Description
Public | Private	Optional. Use `Public` to indicate that the property is available outside the current module or `Private` to indicate the property can only be accessed from other procedures in the current module.

(continued)

Argument	Description
Static	Optional. Indicates that all variables declared inside the property procedure are treated as static variables (their values are preserved between calls to the property procedure). If omitted, all variables declared inside the property procedure are treated non-statically.
name	The name of the property.
arglist	Optional. A list of arguments and their data types that must follow the syntax specified in the definition of the Function statement.
type	Optional. The data type of the return value. If omitted, the return value is typed as a Variant. If the module also contains a Property Let procedure of the same name, the data type of the return value of the Property Get procedure must match the data type of the last parameter of the corresponding Property Let procedure.
statements	Optional. One or more VBA statements.
expression	Optional. The return value of the property procedure. If no "name = expression" statement is included, the return value defaults to the default value of the return value (which depends upon the data type of the return value).
Exit Property	Optional. Causes the property procedure to be immediately exited.

Example: This Property Get procedure, which must be created in a class or form module, returns the elapsed time by calling a private function, GetTime (not shown here). It creates a read-only property because there is no corresponding Property Let procedure:

```
Public Property Get ElapsedTime() As Double
    ElapsedTime = GetTime()
End Property
```

Notes: You can create a property in a class or form module either by using a public variable or by creating property procedures. While declaring and using a public variable is much simpler, the use of property procedures has a couple of advantages:

✦ You can create read-only or write-only properties.

✦ You can do more than simply set or retrieve the value of a variable.

Property Let (Statement)

Description: Creates a procedure in a class module that assigns the value of a property.

Syntax:

```
[Public | Private] [Static] Property Let name
    ([arglist], value)
    [statements]
    [Exit Property]
    [statements]
End Function
```

Argument	Description
Public | Private	Optional. Use Public to indicate that the property is available outside the current module or Private to indicate the property can be accessed only from other procedures in the current module.
Static	Optional. Indicates that all variables declared inside the property procedure are treated as static variables. (Their values are preserved between calls to the property procedure.) If omitted, all variables declared inside the property procedure are treated non-statically.
name	The name of the property. If you wish for the property to be read/write, this name must match the name of a corresponding Property Get procedure.
arglist	Optional. A list of arguments and their data types that must follow the syntax specified in the definition of the Function statement.
value	The name of a variable that holds the value that is assigned to the property by the calling procedure. If the module also contains a Property Get procedure of the same name, the data type of value must match the data type of the return value of the corresponding Property Get procedure.
statements	Optional. One or more VBA statements.
Exit Property	Optional. Causes the property procedure to be immediately exited.

Example: This Property Let procedure, which must be created in a class or form module, sets the value of the customer's name by calling a private function, NameFixUp (not shown here):

```
Public Property Let Name(Value As String)
    Call NameFixUp(pstrName, Value)
End Property
```

Notes: You can create a property in a class or form module either by using a public variable or by creating property procedures.

(*See also* the description of the Property Get statement in this part for more details.)

A property may have one Get Procedure and either a Let or Set Property procedure. Use a Let Property procedure when the property is a simple variable. Use a Set Property procedure when the property is an object.

Property Set (Statement)

Description: Creates a procedure in a class module that sets a property to point to an object.

Syntax:
```
[Public | Private] [Static] Property Set name
    ([arglist], reference)
    [statements]
    [Exit Property]
    [statements]
End Function
```

Argument	Description
Public | Private	Optional. Use Public to indicate that the property is available outside the current module or Private to indicate the property can only be accessed from other procedures in the current module.
Static	Optional. Indicates that all variables declared inside the property procedure are treated as static variables (their values are preserved between calls to the property procedure). If omitted, all variables declared inside the property procedure are treated non-statically.
name	The name of the property. If you wish for the property to be read/write, this name must match the name of a corresponding Property Get procedure.
arglist	Optional. A list of arguments and their data types that must follow the syntax specified in the definition of the Function statement.
reference	The name of a variable that will hold the object reference made by the calling procedure. If the module also contains a Property Get procedure of the same name, the data type of reference must match the data type of the return value of the corresponding Property Get procedure.
statements	Optional. One or more VBA statements.
Exit Property	Optional. Causes the property procedure to be immediately exited.

Example: This Property Set procedure for a class,
clsKitchen, **creates a Parent object of type** clsHouse:

```
Private pobjParent As clsHouse

Public Property Set Parent(objParent As clsHouse)
    If pobjParent Is Nothing Then
        Set pobjParent = New clsHouse
    End If
End Property
```

Notes: A property may have one Get Procedure and either a Let
or Set Property procedure. Use a Let Property procedure when
the property is a simple variable. Use a Set Property procedure
when the property is an object.

Sub (Statement)

Description: Creates a subroutine in the current module.

Syntax:
```
[Public | Private] [Static] Sub name [(arglist)]
    [statements]
    [Exit Sub]
    [statements]
End Sub
```

Argument	Description
Public | Private	Optional. Use Public to indicate that the subroutine is available outside the current module or Private to indicate the subroutine can only be called from other procedures in the current module. (For class and form modules, the Public keyword causes VBA to make the subroutine a method of the class.) Defaults to Public.
Static	Optional. Indicates that all variables declared inside the subroutine are treated as static variables (their values are preserved between calls to the subroutine). If omitted, all variables declared inside the subroutine are treated non-statically.
name	The name of the subroutine.
arglist	Optional. A list of arguments and their data types that must follow the syntax specified in the definition of the function statement.
type	Optional. The data type of the return value. If omitted, the return value is typed as a Variant.
statements	Optional. One or more VBA statements.
Exit Sub	Optional. Causes the subroutine to be immediately exited.

TIP

Example: This subroutine has one Integer parameter:

```
Sub NumFun(intX As Integer)
    Select Case intX
        Case 1
            Debug.Print "1"
        Case 2 To 7
            Debug.Print "2 to 7"
      Case Else
            Debug.Print "else"
    End Select
End Sub
```

Notes: You call a subroutine using the `Call` statement. For example:

```
Call NumFun(6)
```

You can also call `NumFun` using this alternate form of the `Call` statement:

```
NumFun 6
```

In general, if your procedure needs to return something to the calling procedure, you should use a function instead of a subroutine.

Part XII

String Manipulation

In many VBA applications, you need to manipulate strings; fortunately, VBA is quite adept at this. VBA has built-in functions that can return portions of strings, find strings inside other strings, and trim off leading and/or trailing spaces. In this part, you also find VBA keywords to control how string comparisons should be handled (case-sensitive or insensitive) and for converting strings from one variety to another.

Of note, VBA has several keywords that deal with strings (`Asc`, `Chr`, and `Format` come to mind) that I've placed in Part IV instead of this part because of their conversion capabilities. (Hey, it was a tough call because some keywords can be used for multiple purposes.)

In this part . . .

✔ Converting a string to upper or lowercase

✔ Finding a string within another string

✔ Returning some portion of a string

✔ Filling a string with a specified number of any single character

✔ Trimming spaces from a string

✔ Finding the length of a string

✔ Comparing two strings for equality

Keyword Summary

Task	Keyword	Keyword Type
Change a string to lowercase string	LCase	Function
Change a string to uppercase string	UCase	Function
Change a string's character set or case	StrConv	Function
Compare two strings for binary or text equality	StrComp	Function
Fill a string with a specified number of any single character	String	Function
Fill a string with a specified number of spaces	Space	Function
Determine the length of a string	Len	Function
Determine the starting position of a substring within a string	InStr	Function
Left-align a string	LSet	Statement
Replace a portion of a string with another string	Mid	Statement
Return a portion of a string starting at an arbitrary location	Mid	Function
Return the leftmost characters of a string	Left	Function
Return the rightmost characters of a string	Right	Function
Right-align a string	RSet	Statement
Specify the case-sensitivity of string comparisons	Option Compare	Statement
Trim both the leading and trailing spaces from a string	Trim	Function
Trim the leading spaces from a string	LTrim	Function
Trim the trailing spaces from a string	RTrim	Function

InStr (Function)

Description: Returns the starting position of a substring within a string.

Syntax:

```
InStr ( [start,] string1, string2 [, compare] )
```

Parameter	Description
start	Optional. Numeric expression that specifies the starting position within string1 to search for string2. Start is required if compare is specified. Defaults to 1.
string1	The string to search.
string2	The substring to search for within string1.
compare	Optional. Constant that controls how comparisons are made. If omitted, defaults to the Option Compare setting. (If the module doesn't contain an Option Compare statement, defaults to a case-sensitive comparison.) Can be one of the following:

Constant	Value	Description
vbBinaryCompare	0	Perform a binary (case-sensitive) comparison.
vbTextCompare	1	Perform a text (case-insensitive) comparison.
vbDatabaseCompare	2	Perform comparisons based on the database sort order. (Used with Microsoft Access only.)

InStr returns a value based on the following:

If	InStr **Returns**
string2 is found	starting position of substring
string2 is not found	0
string1 is zero-length	0
string2 is zero-length	start (or 1 if start not specified)
string1 or string2 is Null	Null
start is greater than length of string1	0

Example: In the following example, lngPos will return 1:

```
lngPos = Instr(1,"The quick brown fox", _
  "the", vbTextCompare)
```

Notes: If string2 occurs more than once in string1, InStr returns the starting position of the first occurrence (starting with the start position, if start is specified).

LCase (Function)

Description: Returns a string whose characters have been converted to lowercase.

Syntax:

LCase (*string*)

Argument	Description
string	Any valid string expression. If Null, Null is returned.

Example:

strColor = LCase("Blue-GREEN") '= "blue-green"

Notes: A related function, UCase, converts a string to uppercase.

Left (Function)

Description: Returns the leftmost characters of a string.

Syntax:

Left (*string*, *length*)

Argument	Description
string	A string expression. If Null, Null is returned.
length	A numeric expression of type Long indicating the number of characters to return. If zero, a zero-length string is returned. If greater than the length of string, the entire string is returned.

Example:

lngFirst5 = Left("this is a string", 4) '= "this"

Len (Function)

Description: Returns the length of a string.

Syntax:

Len (*expression*)

Argument	Description
expression	A string expression. If Null, Null is returned.

Example:
```
lngChars = Len("The quick brown fox")  '= 19
```

LSet (Statement)

Description: When used with strings, left-aligns the string within a string variable. When used with a user-defined types, copies a variable from one user-defined type to another.

Syntax: The syntax of the string form of LSet is:

```
LSet stringvar = string
```

The syntax of the user-defined type form of LSet is:

```
LSet varname1 = varname2
```

Argument	Description
stringvar	Name of string variable.
string	A string expression to be left-aligned in stringvar.
varname1	Name of variable of a user-defined type which is the target of the copy. varname1 can't contain variable-length strings, objects, or variants.
varname2	Name of variable of a user-defined type that is the source of the copy. varname2 can't contain variable-length strings, objects, or variants.

Example: Here's an example of the first form of LSet:

```
strStuff = "an existing string"
LSet strStuff = "other"   '= "other"
```

Here's an example of the second form of LSet. This example copies all of the data from empOne (of type Employee) to supTwo (of type Supervisor):

```
'the type declarations must occur
'in the Declarations section of a module
Type Employee
    strFirst As String * 10
    strLast As String * 10
End Type
Type Supervisor
    strFirst As String * 10
    strLast As String * 10
End Type
'...
'the rest of the code must occur in a procedure
Dim empOne As Employee
Dim supTwo As Supervisor
```

```
With empOne
    .strFirst = "Mary"
    .strLast = "Chin"
End With
LSet supTwo = empOne
```

Notes: Use RSet to right-align a string within a string variable.

The second form of LSet copies data from elements of the one user-defined type to another without checking for data types or the sizes of the elements. Thus, you should use LSet only with two user-defined types that match exactly in the type, size, and order of elements.

LTrim (Function)

Description: Trims the leading spaces from a string.

Syntax:

LTrim (*string*)

Argument	Description
string	A string expression. If Null, Null is returned.

Example:

```
str0 = "  Hello  "
str1 = ">" & str0 & "<"            ' = ">  Hello  <"
str2 = ">" & LTrim(str0) & "<"  ' = ">Hello  <"
```

Mid (Function)

Description: Returns a portion of a string starting at an arbitrary position.

Syntax:

Mid (*string, start* [, *length*])

Argument	Description
string	A string expression. If Null, Null is returned.
start	A numeric expression of type Long indicating the position in string at which to begin.
length	Optional. A numeric expression of type Long indicating the number of characters to return. If zero, a zero-length string is returned. If greater than the remaining length of string or if omitted, the remainder of the string is returned.

Example:
```
lngMid3 = Mid("this is a string", 9, 3) '= "a s"
```

Mid (Statement)

Description: Replaces a portion of a string with another string

Syntax:
```
Mid ( stringvar, start [, length] ) = string
```

Argument	Description
stringvar	A string variable. If equal to Null or a zero-length string, an error is generated.
start	A numeric expression of type Long indicating the position in stringvar at which to begin replacing text.
length	Optional. A numeric expression of type Long indicating the number of characters to replace. If zero, no replacement is performed. If greater than the length of the replacement string or if omitted, the entire replacement string is used.
string	A string expression that replaces a portion of stringvar.

Example: This example replaces the "his" substring in strStuff with "her":
```
strStuff = "We played with his ball"
Mid(strStuff, InStr(strStuff, "his"), 3) = "her"
'strStuff now equals "We played with her ball'
```

Option Compare (Statement)

Description: Specifies the case sensitivity of string comparisons for a module.

Syntax:
```
Option Compare method
```

Argument	Description
method	May be Binary to indicate that all string comparisons in the module should be binary (case-sensitive); Text to indicate that all string comparisons in the module should be text (case-insensitive); or Database to indicate that all string comparisons in the module should be based on the database sort order. The Database setting may only be used with Microsoft Access.

Example:

All string comparisons in this module will be case-insensitive:

```
'place this statement in the Declarations
'section of a module
Option Compare Text.
```

Notes: If a module doesn't contain an Option Compare state-ment, comparisons are binary (case-sensitive). (Except in Microsoft Access, because Access automatically inserts Option Compare Database into each new module.)

Right (Function)

Description: Returns the rightmost characters of a string.

Syntax:

```
Left ( string, length )
```

Argument	Description
string	A string expression. If Null, Null is returned.
length	A numeric expression of type Long indicating the number of characters to return. If zero, a zero-length string is returned. If greater than the length of string, the entire string is returned.

Example:

```
lngLast5 = Right("this is a string", 5) '= "tring"
```

RSet (Statement)

Description: Right-aligns a string within a string variable.

Syntax:

```
RSet stringvar = string
```

Argument	Description
stringvar	Name of string variable.
string	A string expression to be right-aligned in stringvar.

Example:

```
strStuff = "an existing string"
RSet strStuff = "other"    '= "                    other"
```

Notes: Use LSet to left-align a string within a string variable.

RTrim (Function)

Description: Trims the trailing spaces from a string.

Syntax:

RTrim (*string*)

Argument	Description
string	A string expression. If Null, Null is returned.

Example:

```
str0 = "  Hello  "
str1 = ">" & str0 & "<"          '= ">  Hello  <"
str3 = ">" & RTrim(str0) & "<" '= ">  Hello<"
```

Space (Function)

Description: Returns a string made up of a specified number of spaces.

Syntax:

Space (*number*)

Argument	Description
number	A numeric expression of type Long indicating the number of spaces to include in the return string.

Example:

```
strSpaced = Space(10) '= "          "
```

Notes: A related function, String, returns a string filled with a specified number of any single character.

StrComp (Function)

Description: Compares two strings for binary or text equality.

Syntax:

StrComp (*string1, string2* [, *compare*])

Argument	Description
string1	A valid string expression to compare with string2.
string2	A valid string expression to compare with string1.
compare	Constant that controls how comparisons are made. If omitted, defaults to the Option Compare setting. Can be one of the constants specified in the definition of the InStr function:

StrComp returns a value based on the following:

If	InStr **Returns**
string1 is equal to string2	0
string1 is (alphabetically) less than string2	-1
string1 is (alphabetically) greater than string2	1
string1 or string2 is Null	Null

Example: In these examples: intcomp1=1 and intComp 2=0:

```
intCompl = StrComp("abc", "ABC", vbBinaryCompare)
intComp2 = StrComp("abc", "ABC", vbTextCompare)
```

StrConv (Function)

Description: Changes a string's character set or case.

Syntax:

```
StrConv ( string, conversion )
```

Argument	Description
string	A valid string expression.
conversion	An Integer value that indicates the type of conversion to perform. Can be one or more of the following constants (to use more than one setting, add the settings together):

Constant	Value	Description
vbUpperCase	1	Converts the string to uppercase characters.
vbLowerCase	2	Converts the string to lowercase characters.
vbProperCase	3	Converts the first character of every word in the string to uppercase and every other character to lowercase.

Constant	Value	Description
vbWide	4	Converts narrow (single-byte) characters in the string to wide (double-byte) characters. (Applies only to Far East versions.)
vbNarrow	8	Converts wide (double-byte) characters in the string to narrow (single-byte) characters. (Applies only to Far East versions.)
vbKatakana	16	Converts Hiragana characters in the string to Katakana characters. (Applies only to Japanese versions.)
vbHiragana	16	Converts Katakana characters in the string to Hiragana characters. (Applies only to Japanese versions.)
vbUnicode	64	Converts the string to Unicode using the default code page of the system.
vbFromUnicode	128	Converts the string from Unicode to the default code page of the system.

Example: The following example returns "Hello There K9ki":

```
strCnv = StrConv("HELLO there k9KI",vbProperCase)
```

Notes: When you convert a string to proper case using StrConv, the following characters are considered word separators: Null (Chr(0)), horizontal and vertical tab (Chr(9) and Chr(11)), linefeed (Chr(10)), form feed (Chr(12)), carriage return (Chr(13)), space (Chr(32) for single-byte character systems; varies for double-byte character systems).

String (Function)

Description: Returns a string filled with a specified number of any single character.

Syntax:

```
String ( number, character )
```

Argument	Description
number	A numeric expression of type Long indicating the number of spaces to include in the return string.
character	ANSI character code of string to repeat or a string expression. If a string expression, only the first character repeats.

Example:

```
strStrung1 = String(10, "x")  '= "xxxxxxxxxx"
strStrung2 = String(4, 37)    '= "%%%%"
```

Trim (Function)

Description: Trims both leading and trailing spaces from a string.

Syntax:

```
Trim ( string )
```

Argument	Description
string	A string expression. If Null, Null is returned.

Example:

```
str0 = "  Hello  "
str1 = ">" & str0 & "<"         '= ">  Hello  <"
str4 = ">" & Trim(str0) & "<"   '= ">Hello<"
```

UCase (Function)

Description: Returns a string whose characters have been converted to uppercase.

Syntax:

```
UCase ( string )
```

Argument	Description
string	Any valid string expression. If Null, Null is returned.

Example:

```
strColor = UCase("Blue-GREEN") '= "BLUE-GREEN"
```

Notes: A related function, LCase, converts a string to lowercase.

Part XIII

User Forms

The VBA IDE includes a forms package, alternately called in the documentation *User Forms* and *Microsoft Forms.* (Who said Microsoft had to be consistent?) The forms package is real useful for doing all sorts of formsy stuff. You can place controls on these forms and use the forms to collect and display data. The keywords in this part show you how to manipulate these forms from your VBA code. If the User Forms object model interests you, then check out Part XV.

For Microsoft Access users, be aware that Access uses a different forms package that differs significantly from User Forms — none of the keywords in this part will work with Access forms.

In this part . . .

- ✔ **Loading and displaying forms**
- ✔ **Hiding forms**
- ✔ **Unloading forms**
- ✔ **Printing forms**

Keyword Summary

Task	Keyword	Keyword Type
Hide a form without unloading it	Hide	Method
Load and display a form	Show	Method
Load a form into memory without displaying it	Load	Statement
Print an image of a form to the printer	PrintForm	Method
Unload a form and completely remove it from memory	Unload	Statement

Hide (Method)

Definition: Hides a form without unloading it.

Syntax:

`[object.]Hide`

Parameter	Description
object	Optional. The name of a currently loaded user form. If the code is executing from the form's module, you may use the Me object to refer to the current form object. In fact, when executed from the form's module, you can completely leave off the object reference (and the dot) to hide the current form.

Example: All three of these statements hide a form named frmOrder if executed from code contained in frmOrder's module. Only the first statement, however, hides frmOrder from code that lives in some other module.

```
frmOrder.Hide
Me.Hide
Hide
```

Notes: The Hide method does not unload the form from memory. To unload the form, use the Unload statement. To display the hidden form, use the Show method.

Load (Statement)

Definition: Loads a form into memory without making it visible.

Syntax:

`Load object`

Argument	Description
object	The name of a user form.

Example: This example loads `frmOrder` without displaying it:

```
Load frmOrder
```

Notes: To display a form loaded using the `Load` statement, you must use the form's `Show` method.

You can use the `Load` statement to preload a form. Then when you later use the `Show` method to display the preloaded form, the form displays faster than if the form hadn't been preloaded.

PrintForm (Method)

Definition: Prints an image of a form to the printer.

Syntax:

```
[object.]PrintForm
```

Argument	Description
object	Optional. The name of a currently loaded user form. If the code is executing from the form's module, you may use the `Me` object to refer to the current form object. In fact, when executed from the form's module, you can completely leave off the object reference (and the dot) to print the current form.

Example: frmOrder.PrintForm

Show (Method)

Definition: Loads and displays a form.

Syntax:

```
[object.]Show
```

Parameter	Description
object	The name of a user form. If the code executes from the form's module, you may use the `Me` object to refer to the current form object. When executed from the form's module — perhaps from the form's `Initialize` event procedure — you can even leave off the object reference (and the dot) to show the current form.

Example: This example loads and displays the `frmCustomer` form:

```
frmCustomer.Show
```

This example preloads `frmClient` but doesn't display it yet:

```
Load frmClient
```

And now it's time to display the preloaded but hidden `frmClient` form:

```
frmClient.Show
```

Unload (Statement)

Definition: Unloads a form and completely removes it from memory.

Syntax:

```
Unload object
```

Argument	Description
object	The name of a user form that is currently loaded.

Example: This example unloads the frmTrackAndField form:

```
Unload frmTrackAndField
```

Notes: After a form unloads, you cannot access the values in any of its controls. If you wish to hide a form but not unload it from memory, use the `Hide` method instead.

Part XIV

Variables and Constants

Variables vary and constants stay constant, but I bet you already knew that! In this part, you find lots of keywords that you can use to create and manipulate variables and constants. Most of these keywords should be familiar to you if you've been using VBA for some time, but some keywords, such as `TypeName` and `Option Private Module`, are fairly obscure.

In this part . . .

- ✓ **Declaring constants**
- ✓ **Declaring variables**
- ✓ **Determining if a** `Variant` **variable is** `Null` **or** `Empty`
- ✓ **Creating user-defined types**
- ✓ **Assigning a value to a variable**
- ✓ **Determining the data type of a variable**
- ✓ **Setting an object variable to point to an object**

Keyword Summary

Task	Keyword	Keyword Type
Assign a value to a variable	`Let`	Statement
Create a user-defined type	`Type`	Statement
Declare a constant	`Const`	Statement
Declare a local static variable	`Static`	Statement
Declare a local variable	`Dim`	Statement
Declare a module as private	`Option Private Module`	Statement
Declare a private variable	`Private`	Statement
Declare a public variable	`Public`	Statement
Declare the default data type for variables starting with a specified range of characters	`Deftype`	Statement
Determine the data type of a variable using a descriptive string	`TypeName`	Function
Determine the subtype of a `Variant` variable	`VarType`	Function
Point an object variable to an object	`Set`	Statement
Require explicit object declaration	`Option Explicit`	Statement
Return an object variable that refers to the class or form in which the code is executing	`Me`	Keyword
Verify if a variable holds an array	`IsArray`	Function
Verify if a variable is an object variable	`IsObject`	Function
Verify if a `Variant` variable has been initialized	`IsEmpty`	Function
Verify if a `Variant` variable is set to `Null`	`IsNull`	Function
Verify if an expression can be evaluated as a date	`IsDate`	Function
Verify if an expression can be evaluated as a number	`IsNumeric`	Function
Verify if an expression is set to an error value	`IsError`	Function
Verify if an optional argument was passed to a procedure	`IsMissing`	Function

Const (Statement)

Description: Declares a constant.

Syntax:

```
[Public | Private] Const constname [As type] =
    expression
```

Argument	Description
Public | Private	Optional. Use Public to indicate that the constant is available outside the current module, or Private to indicate the constant can be accessed only from other procedures in the current module. Defaults to Private. If you use Public, the constant declaration must be located in the Declarations section of a module.
constname	Name of constant.
type	Optional. The data type of the constant. May be one of the following: Byte, Boolean, Integer, Long, Currency, Single, Double, Date, String, or Variant. Defaults to the most appropriate data type for the expression.
expression	An expression made up of a literal string or numeric value, another constant, and any arithmetic or logical operator (except for Is).

Example: This example defines a local numeric constant:

```
Const PI = 3.14159
```

This example defines a public string constant (must be made in the Declarations section of a module):

```
Public Const conBookName As String = _
    "VBA for Dummies Quick Reference"
```

Notes: You can't use variables or intrinsic or user-defined functions in a constant declaration.

Constants declared at the procedure level are always private. Constants declared at the module level (in the Declarations section) can be module-global (using Private) or project-global (using Public). You can't use the Public keyword in procedures or in the Declarations section of a class or form (or in Microsoft Access, in the Declarations section of an Access form or report) module.

Using constants with descriptive names in your code instead of "magic," arbitrary values is a good idea. Descriptive names make your code self documenting and easier to modify.

Deftype (Statement)

Description: Declares the default data type for variables, arguments, and function and property procedure return values for names in the module starting with a specified range of characters.

Syntax:

`Deftype letterrange [,letterrange, ...]`

Argument	Description
`type`	The default data type of variables you wish to declare. May be one of: `Bool, Byte, Cur, Date, Dbl, Dec, Int, Lng, Obj, Sng, Str,` or `Var`.
`letterrange`	A range of alphabetic letters in the form of `letter 1[-letter2]`.

Example: DefInt i-n, z

Notes: Using `Deftype` affects all variable, argument, function, and `Property Get` procedure names in the module. Unless otherwise implicitly declared, these elements have the default data type specified in the `Deftype` statement.

You can override the `Deftype` statement by using explicit data types in your `Dim`, `Static`, `Private`, and `Public` statements.

`Deftype` statements don't affect the data type of elements of user-defined types.

VBA includes the `Deftype` statement for backward compatibility with earlier versions of BASIC. Using the `Deftype` statement is not considered a good programming practice and should be avoided.

Dim (Statement)

Description: `Dim` declares a local (procedure-level) variable when used inside a procedure. When used in the `Declarations` section of a module, `Dim` declares a module-level variable.

Syntax:

```
Dim [WithEvents] varname1[(subscript1)]
[As [New] type1]
[, [WithEvents] varname2[(subscript2)]
[As [New] type2] , ...]
```

Argument	Description
WithEvents	Optional. Specifies that varname is an object variable to be used as an event sink (a way to capture another object's events and respond to them) for an ActiveX object. Cannot be used with arrays or the New keyword. Only valid in class modules. **See also** the Notes section for more on WithEvents.
varname	The name of a variable you wish to declare.
subscripts	Optional. Dimensions of an array variable of the form [lowerbound To] upperbound [, ...]. You can specify up to 60 multiple dimensions. If you omit the lowerbound, VBA uses a lowerbound of 0 (or 1 if you've used the Option Base 1 statement).
New	Optional. Implicitly creates an instance of an object. If you use New when declaring an object variable, VBA implicitly instantiates the object the first time you attempt to set or get a property of the object or execute a method of the object. This works with both class module objects and certain Automation objects.
type	Optional. Data type of the variable. May be Byte, Boolean, Integer, Long, Currency, Single, Double, Date, String, String*length (for fixed-length strings), Object, Variant, a user-defined type, or a specific Automation or class module object type. Defaults to Variant.

Example: This example creates a simple string variable:

```
Dim strFirstName As String
```

This example creates a fixed 2-dimensional array of 1000 (10 x 100) strings:

```
Dim strNames(1 To 100, 1 To 10) As String
```

This example creates an event sink variable, objWord, that will respond to events of Word's application object:

```
Dim WithEvents objWord As Word.Application
```

Notes: See also Part III for a more thorough discussion of arrays.

When used in the Declarations section of a module, Dim is equivalent to the Private statement.

When you declare a numeric variable, it initializes to a default value of 0. A String variable initializes to a default value of a zero-length string. A Variant variable initializes to a default value of Empty.

After you declare an event sink object variable using the WithEvents keyword and compile the project, you'll notice that the VBA IDE Object dropdown box now includes an entry for the object, and the VBA IDE Procedures dropdown box now includes entries for the events the ActiveX object exposes for event sinking. This allows you to create code that runs when the ActiveX object fires these "sinked" events.

Although not required, placing all Dim statements at the beginning of your procedures is wise. Also, do not depend upon implicit variable declaration. *See also* the definition of Option Explicit for more details.

IsArray (Function)

Description: Returns a Boolean indicating if the variable is an array.

Syntax:

```
IsArray ( variable )
```

Argument	Description
variable	Name of variable.

Example:

```
Dim strFruits() As String
Dim strApple As String
fIsIt = IsArray(strFruits) ' fIsIt = True
fIsIt = IsArray(strApple)  ' fIsIt = False
```

Notes: IsArray returns True for dynamic and fixed-size arrays, as well as arrays created with the Array statement.

IsDate (Function)

Description: Returns a Boolean indicating if the expression *can* be evaluated as a VBA date.

Syntax:

```
IsDate ( expression )
```

Argument	Description
expression	A Variant or String expression.

Example:

```
strStuff1 = "April 25, 1998"
intStuff2 = 4
varStuff3 = "11/28/99"
strStuff4 = "8-Jan-1992"
```

```
varStuff5 = "12:04"
fIsDate1 = IsDate(strStuff1)   '= True
fIsDate2 = IsDate(intStuff2)   '= False
fIsDate3 = IsDate(varStuff3)   '= True
fIsDate4 = IsDate(strStuff4)   '= True
fIsDate5 = IsDate(varStuff5)   '= True
```

Notes: IsDate does not determine if the expression *is* a date variable as the examples illustrate; instead IsDate determines if the expression *can* be converted into a date/time variable. **See also** Part V for more on dates.

IsEmpty (Function)

Description: Returns a Boolean indicating if a Variant variable has been initialized.

Syntax:

IsEmpty (*expression*)

Argument	Description
expression	A Variant expression.

Example:

```
Dim varOne As Variant
Dim varTwo As Variant
Dim varThree As Variant
Dim fIsEmpty1 As Boolean
Dim fIsEmpty2 As Boolean
Dim fIsEmpty3 As Boolean
varOne = "hello"
varThree = "hello"
varThree = Empty
fIsEmpty1 = IsEmpty(varOne)    '= False
fIsEmpty2 = IsEmpty(varTwo)    '= True
fIsEmpty3 = IsEmpty(varThree)  '= True
```

Notes: Variant variables all start out as Empty. After you assign them a value, however, they are no longer Empty unless you assign them to the special Empty keyword or to another Empty variable. Empty is *not* the same as Null.

IsError (Function)

Description: Returns a Boolean indicating if an expression is set to an error value.

Syntax:

IsEmpty (*expression*)

Argument	Description
expression	A Variant expression.

Example:

```
varOne = "hello"
varTwo = CVErr(34565)
fIsError1 = IsError(varOne)      '= False
fIsError2 = IsError(varTwo)      '= True
```

Notes: Error values are created using the CVErr function, which is discussed in Part VI.

IsMissing (Function)

Description: Returns a Boolean indicating if an optional argument was passed a value.

Syntax:

IsMissing (*argname*)

Argument	Description
argname	The name of an optional Variant argument to the procedure.

Example: You may use this function to maintain an incrementing counter. If you call Increment without any argument, the counter is incremented by 1; otherwise it's incremented by the value of varInc:

```
Function Increment(Optional varIncr As Variant)
    Static slngTotal As Variant
    If IsMissing(varIncr) Then varIncr = 1
    slngTotal = slngTotal + varIncr
    Increment = slngTotal
End Function
```

Notes: You can use IsMissing with both Variant and specifically typed optional arguments.

IsNull (Function)

Description: Returns a Boolean indicating if an expression is set to Null.

Syntax:

IsNull (*expression*)

Argument	Description
expression	A Variant expression.

Example:

```
Dim varOne As Variant
Dim varTwo As Variant
Dim varThree As Variant
Dim fIsNull1 As Boolean
Dim fIsNull2 As Boolean
Dim fIsNull3 As Boolean
varOne = "hello"
varThree = Null
fIsNull1 = IsNull(varOne)    '= False
fIsNull2 = IsNull(varTwo)    '= False
fIsNull3 = IsNull(varThree)  '= True
```

Notes: Variant variables start out as Empty, which is not the same as Null. You set a Variant variable to Null by assigning it to the special Null keyword, or by assigning it to another variable, object property, or database field that is Null.

IsNumeric (Function)

Description: Returns a Boolean indicating if the expression *can* be evaluated as a number.

Syntax:

IsNumeric (*expression*)

Argument	Description
expression	A Variant or String expression.

Example:

```
varStuff1 = "April 25, 1998"
varStuff2 = "4"
varStuff3 = "albatross"
varStuff4 = 34.89
fIsNumeric1 = IsNumeric(varStuff1)  '= False
fIsNumeric2 = IsNumeric(varStuff2)  '= True
fIsNumeric3 = IsNumeric(varStuff3)  '= False
fIsNumeric4 = IsNumeric(varStuff4)  '= True
```

Notes: IsNumeric does not check if the expression is a numeric variable; instead IsNumeric determines if the expression *can* be converted into a numeric variable.

IsObject (Function)

Description: Returns a Boolean indicating if an identifier represents an object variable.

Syntax:

IsObject (*identifier*)

Argument	Description
identifier	The name of a variable.

Example: This example (which should be run from Microsoft Excel) illustrates the use of IsObject:

```
Dim varStuff As Variant
Dim objDoc As Object
Dim xlwWorkbook As Excel.Workbook
Dim varWorkbook As Variant
Dim fIsObject1 As Boolean
Dim fIsObject2 As Boolean
Dim fIsObject3 As Boolean
Dim fIsObject4 As Boolean
Set varWorkbook = Excel.Workbooks(1)
fIsObject1 = IsObject(varStuff)     '= False
fIsObject2 = IsObject(objDoc)       '= True
fIsObject3 = IsObject(xlwWorkbook)  '= True
fIsObject4 = IsObject(varWorkbook)  '= True
```

Notes: As is illustrated in the examples, IsObject returns True for variables declared as either generic object or specific variables. IsObject also returns True for Variant variables that have been set to point to objects.

Let (Statement)

Description: Assigns a value to a variable.

Syntax:

[Let] *varname* = *expression*

Argument	Description
varname	The name of a variable or property.
expression	An expression whose value you wish to assign to varname.

Example:
```
Let intX = 5
strFirstName = "Paul"
intValue = CInt(34.59)
```

Notes: VBA automatically converts the expression to the datatype of `varname` when executing the `Let` statement. If you want more control on how this conversion is made, you should use one of the VBA conversion functions as illustrated in the third example. *See also* Part IV for more on conversion functions.

Although the `Let` statement is a very commonly-used VBA statement, you rarely, if ever, see `Let` statements that use the optional `Let` keyword. Most programmers omit the `Let` keyword.

Me (Keyword)

Description: Returns an implicitly-declared object variable that refers to the class or form from which the code is currently executing.

Syntax:

`Me`

Example: This statement hides a form if executed from code contained in the form's module:

`Me.Hide`

Notes: Me is valid only in a form or class module (in Microsoft Access, Me is also valid in a report module). If used in a standard module, it causes a compile-time error.

Option Explicit (Statement)

Description: Requires explicit variable declarations for the module.

Syntax:

`Option Explicit`

Example:
```
'place this in the Declarations section of a module
Option Explicit
```

Notes: If `Option Explicit` does not appear in the `Declarations` section of a module, VBA lets you use variables that you haven't declared. This is a bad idea because it greatly increases the probability that your code will have bugs caused by variable name misspellings. Every module should include an Option Explicit statement!

I highly recommended you check the Require Variable Declaration checkbox found on the Editor tab (the Module tab in Microsoft Access) of the Options dialog box (select Tools⇨Options). When you do this, VBA automatically inserts an Option Explicit statement into the Declarations section of every new module. (It doesn't change existing modules, however.)

Option Private Module (Statement)

Description: When used in VBA hosts that allow cross-project references, Option Private Module prevents such references. When used in VBA hosts that don't allow cross-project references, it has no effect.

Syntax:

```
Option Private Module
```

Example:

```
'place this in the Declarations section of a module
Option Private Module
```

Notes: Microsoft Excel is an example of a VBA host that allows cross-project references.

Private (Statement)

Description: Declares a module-level variable in the Declarations section of a module.

Syntax:

```
Private [WithEvents] varname1[(subscript1)]
[As [New] type1]
[, [WithEvents] varname2[(subscript2)]
[As [New] type2] , ...]
```

See the definition of the Dim statement for a description of these arguments.

Example: This example creates a module-level string variable:

```
Private mstrFirstName As String
```

This example creates a module-level fixed 2-dimensional array of 1000 (10 x 100) strings:

```
Private mstrNames(1 To 100, 1 To 10) As String
```

Notes: See also Part III for a more thorough discussion of arrays.

The `Private` statement may not be used inside a procedure. When used in the `Declarations` section of a module, `Dim` is equivalent to the `Private` statement.

See also the notes under the definition of the `Dir` statement.

Public (Statement)

Description: Declares a project-level variable in the `Declarations` section of a module.

Syntax:
```
Public [WithEvents] varname1[(subscript1)]
[As [New] type1]
[, [WithEvents] varname2[(subscript2)]
[As [New] type2] , ...]
```

See the definition of the `Dim` statement for a description of these arguments.

Example: This example creates a project-level string variable:
```
Public gstrFirstName As String
```

This example creates a static 2-dimensional public array of 1000 (10 x 100) strings:
```
Dim gstrNames(1 To 100, 1 To 10) As String
```

Notes: See also Part III for a more thorough discussion of arrays.

When you declare public variables for class modules, they become properties of the class module objects.

See also the notes under the definition of the `Dir` statement.

Set (Statement)

Description: Assigns an object variable or property to point to an object.

Syntax:
```
Set objectvar = [New] objectexpression
```

Argument	Description
objectvar	An object variable or property that allows for object references.

Argument	Description
New	Optional. Creates a new instance of a class or Automation object.
objectexpression	Expression consisting of name of object, another object variable of the same object type, a function or method that returns an object reference, or the Nothing keyword. The Nothing keyword removes the reference to an object and releases resources associated with a previously referenced object if no other object variable refers to the object.

Example: This example creates an Automation object variable that points to an Excel Application object using the CreateObject function:

```
Dim objExcel As Object
Set objExcel = CreateObject("Excel.Application")
```

This example creates a new instance of the clsStopwatch class:

```
Dim objTimer As clsStopwatch
Set objTimer = New clsStopwatch
```

Static (Statement)

Description: Declares a local (procedure-level) variable that retains its value between procedure calls.

Syntax:

```
Static varname1[(subscript1)] [As [New] type1]
[, varname2[(subscript2)] [As [New] type2] , ...]
```

See the definition of the Dim statement for a description of these arguments.

Example: This example creates a simple static string variable:

```
Static strFirstName As String
```

This example creates a static fixed 2-dimensional array of 1000 (10 x 100) strings:

```
Static strNames(1 To 100, 1 To 10) As String
```

Notes: See also Part III for a more thorough discussion of arrays.

Static is only valid within a procedure.

If you use the Static keyword in the Function or Sub statement, all variables within the procedure declared using a Dim statement are static. *See also* Part XI for more details.

Using a `Static` variable instead of a module-level or project-level global variable is a good idea.

See also the notes under the definition of the `Dir` statement.

Type (Statement)

Description: Creates a user-defined data type.

Syntax:

```
[Private | Public] Type typename
    elementname-1 [(subscripts-1)] As type1
    ...
    elementname-n  [(subscripts-n)] As typen
End Type
```

Argument	Description
Public | Private	Optional. Use `Public` to indicate that the user-defined type is available outside the current module or `Private` to indicate the user-defined type can only be used from procedures in the current module. Defaults to `Private`.
typename	The name of the user-defined type.
elementname	The name of the element. Types may have as many elements as you'd like.
subscripts	Optional. Dimensions of an array variable element of the form [`lowerbound To`] `upperbound` [`, ...`]. You can specify up to 60 multiple dimensions. If you omit the lowerbound, VBA uses a lowerbound of `0` (or `1` if you've used the `Option Base 1` statement).
type	Optional. Data type of the element. May be `Byte`, `Boolean`, `Integer`, `Long`, `Currency`, `Single`, `Double`, `Date`, `String`, `String*length` (for fixed-length strings), `Object`, `Variant`, a user-defined type, or a specific `Automation` or class module object type. Defaults to `Variant`.

Example: This example illustrates how to create a user-defined type, as well as how to declare a variable as a user-defined type, and how to set the values of such a variable:

```
'Place this Type definition in the
'Declarations section of a module.
Type Grail
    strName As String * 30
    strQuest As String * 50
    strOther As String * 30
    datAnswer As Date
```

```
End Type
'...
Dim recBridgeCrossing As Grail
'...
With recBridgeCrossing
    .strName = "Sir Robin"
    .strQuest = "To seek the holy grail"
    .strOther = "Blue, no green. Ahhhh!"
    .datAnswer = Now()
End With
```

Notes: Type statements must be located in the Declarations section of a module; they can't be placed within a procedure.

User-defined types are useful when using the Get and Put statements to read and write data to text or binary files. While you don't have to use user-defined types with the Get and Put statements, using them can make your life easier. (**See also** Part VII for more details.)

TypeName (Function)

Description: Returns a String describing the data type of a variable expression.

Syntax:

TypeName (*varname*)

Argument	Description
varname	A variable or variable expression. Cannot be a variable of a user-defined type.

TypeName returns a string equal to one of the following:

Return Value	Description
objecttype	An object whose type is objecttype
Byte	Byte value
Integer	Integer
Long	Long integer
Single	Single-precision floating-point number
Double	Double-precision floating-point number
Currency	Currency value
Decimal	Decimal value
Date	Date value
String	String

Return Value	Description
Boolean	Boolean value
Error	An error value
Empty	Uninitialized variable
Null	Null value
Object	An object
Unknown	An object whose type is unknown
Nothing	Object variable that doesn't refer to an object

Example:

```
Dim varOne As Variant
Dim varTwo As Variant
Dim strType1 As String
Dim strType2 As String
Dim strType3 As String
Dim strType4 As String
Dim strType5 As String
Dim avarAges(1 To 5) As Variant
varOne = "howdy"
varTwo = Null
avarAges(1) = 4
strType1 = TypeName(varOne)        '= String
strType2 = TypeName(varTwo)        '= Null
strType3 = TypeName(1234.57)       '= Double
strType4 = TypeName(avarAges)      '= Variant()
strType5 = TypeName(avarAges(1))   '= Integer
```

Notes: If varname is an array, TypeName returns the data type of the whole array (as declared) appended to an empty set of parentheses. If varname is an element of the array, TypeName returns the actual data type of the element. This is illustrated by the last two examples.

A related function, VarType, returns an Integer indicating the data type of an expression.

VarType (Function)

Description: Returns an Integer indicating the subtype of a Variant variable.

Syntax:

VarType (*varname*)

Argument	Description
varname	A variable or variable expression. Cannot be a variable of a user-defined type.

VarType returns an Integer equal to one of the following:

Constant	Value	Description
vbEmpty	0	Empty (uninitialized)
vbNull	1	Null
vbInteger	2	Integer
vbLong	3	Long integer
vbSingle	4	Single-precision floating-point number
vbDouble	5	Double-precision floating-point number
vbCurrency	6	Currency value
vbDate	7	Date value
vbString	8	String
vbObject	9	Object
vbError	10	Error value
vbBoolean	11	Boolean value
vbVariant	12	Variant (used only with arrays of variants)
vbDataObject	13	A data access object
vbDecimal	14	Decimal value
vbByte	17	Byte value
vbArray	8192	Array (plus the data type of the array)

Example:

```
Dim varOne As Variant
Dim varTwo As Variant
Dim intType1 As Integer
Dim intType2 As Integer
Dim intType3 As Integer
Dim intType4 As Integer
Dim intType5 As Integer
Dim avarAges(1 To 5) As Variant
varOne = "howdy"
varTwo = Null
avarAges(1) = 4
intType1 = VarType(varOne)          '= 8
intType2 = VarType(varTwo)          '= 1
intType3 = VarType(1234.57)         '= 5
intType4 = VarType(avarAges)        '= 8204 (8192 +
   12)
intType5 = VarType(avarAges(1))     '= 2
```

Notes: A related function, TypeName, returns a String indicating the data type of an expression.

Microsoft Office 97 Object Models

In order for your VBA code to interact with and control your host environment, you must understand the relationships between the host's objects. The host environment's object model visually represents these relationships. For example, the object model in Excel tells you that the Excel application contains a workbooks collection that contains all of the currently open workbook objects, each of which contains a worksheets collection, which in turn contains all of the workbook's worksheets, and so on. Programming an application's objects without an object model is like exploring a foreign country without a map — it's possible, but only for the truly adventurous.

Object models are also useful if you plan to use Automation to control one application from another. For example, you may use code inside of your Access database application to open Word, merge data from the Access database with a Word document, and then print the Word document.

In this part . . .

✔ **Understanding object models**

✔ **Navigating the Microsoft Office object models**

Thirteen Object Models

In this part, you find the object models of the five Microsoft Office 97 applications — Access, Excel, Outlook, PowerPoint, and Word — as well as the object models of eight shared components. While these 13 are the most common object models, this book can't possibly include every object model that every VBA programmer ever will need. If you're using a host program that I haven't included here — such as Visio, Crystal Reports, or Microsoft Map — you need to consult the host product's documentation or online help system.

What about Properties and Methods?

One thing you don't find in the object models in this part are the properties and methods for all of the objects and collections. Remember, this is a quick reference! Fortunately, after you navigate through the object model to the right object, it's easy enough to learn about an object's properties and methods by using VBA's IntelliSense features, the VBA Object Browser, or online help.

Key to the Object Models

collection	This represents a collection (usually plural) of objects (usually singular). In the interest of simplicty, I've only included here the name of the collection. For example, in the Word object model, you find a Documents collection that represents both the collection of Documents as well as the individual Document objects.
object	This represents a single object. For example, in the Excel object model, you find that the Worksheet object contains a Range object. This means that there is no collection of Range objects, only a single Range object per Worksheet.
component...	Sometimes, an object or a collection has a label that is bolded, underlined, and ends with "...". This signifies that this object or collection represents a shared Office component, whose object model is described elsewhere in this Part. For example, many of the Office object models include a reference to the Assistant object whose object model is fully diagrammed elsewhere.
object...	Sometimes, an object or a collection has a label that is bolded, and ends with "..." (with no underline). This signifies that this object model was too big to fit on a single page. This object or collection can be found on another page. For example, in the main PowerPoint object model, you find reference to the Slides collection, which is fully diagrammed on the following page.

Access 97

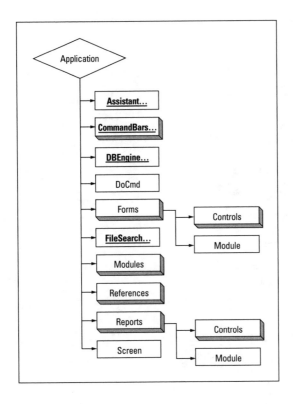

Excel 97

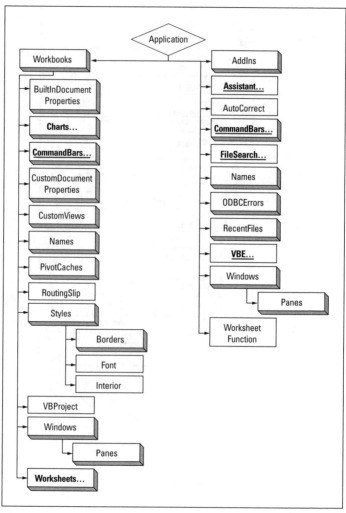

(continued)

(continued)

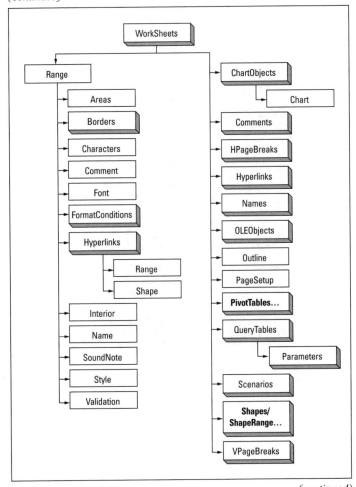

(continued)

(continued)

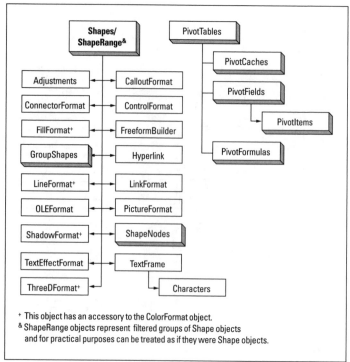

+ This object has an accessory to the ColorFormat object.
& ShapeRange objects represent filtered groups of Shape objects
   and for practical purposes can be treated as if they were Shape objects.

(continued)

(continued)

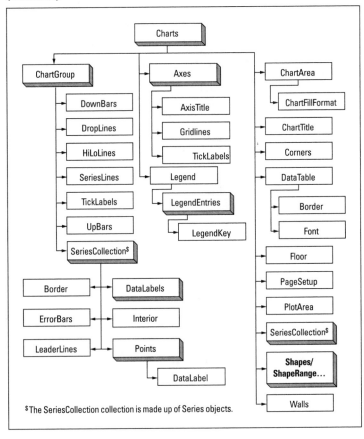

$The SeriesCollection collection is made up of Series objects.

Outlook 97

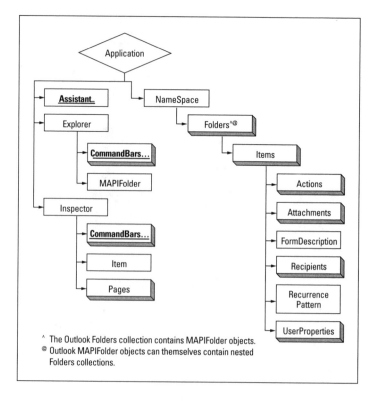

^ The Outlook Folders collection contains MAPIFolder objects.
@ Outlook MAPIFolder objects can themselves contain nested Folders collections.

PowerPoint 97

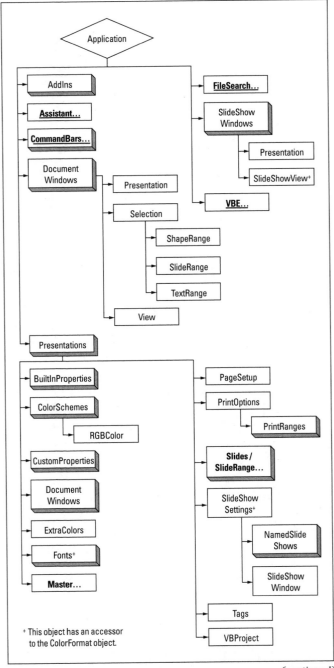

+ This object has an accessor
to the ColorFormat object.

(continued)

(continued)

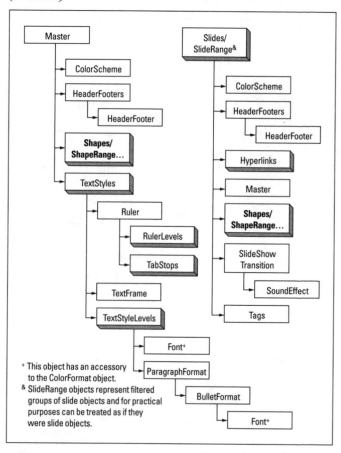

(continued)

(continued)

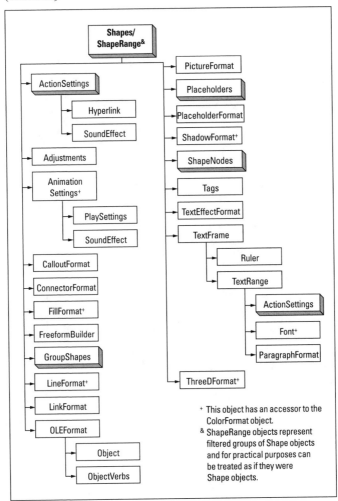

+ This object has an accessor to the
  ColorFormat object.
& ShapeRange objects represent
  filtered groups of Shape objects
  and for practical purposes can
  be treated as if they were
  Shape objects.

Word 97

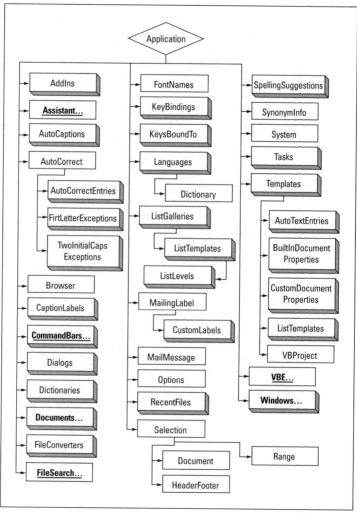

(continued)

(continued)

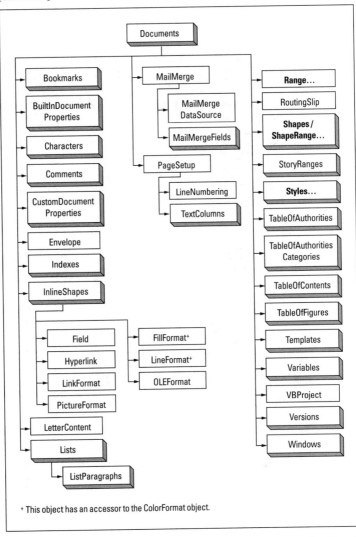

+ This object has an accessor to the ColorFormat object.

(continued)

(continued)

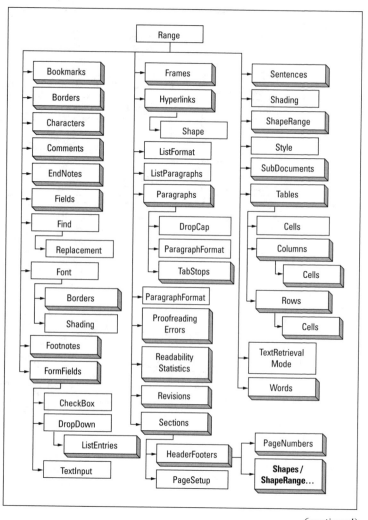

(continued)

(continued)

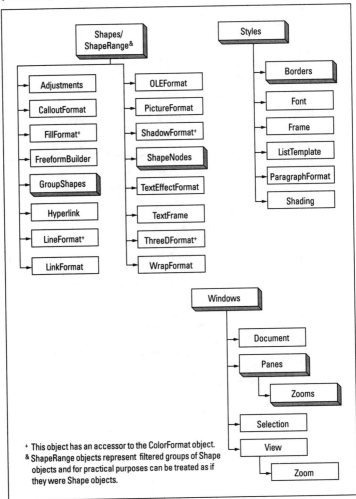

+ This object has an accessor to the ColorFormat object.
& ShapeRange objects represent filtered groups of Shape objects and for practical purposes can be treated as if they were Shape objects.

Data Access Objects 3.5 for Jet Workspaces

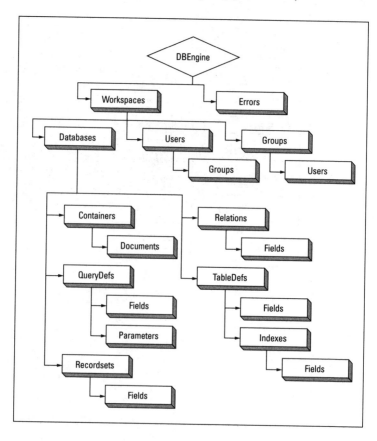

Data Access Objects 3.5 for ODBC Direct

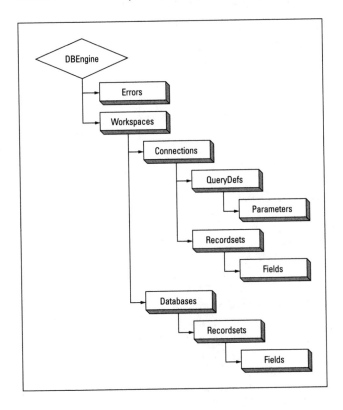

Office Assistant

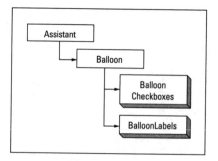

Office Binder

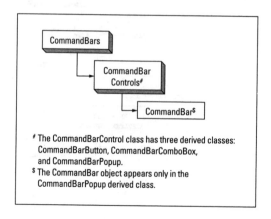

The CommandBarControl class has three derived classes:
CommandBarButton, CommandBarComboBox,
and CommandBarPopup.
$ The CommandBar object appears only in the
CommandBarPopup derived class.

Office Command Bars

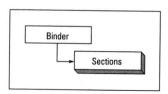

Office FileSearch

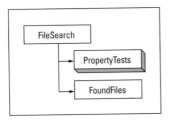

Forms

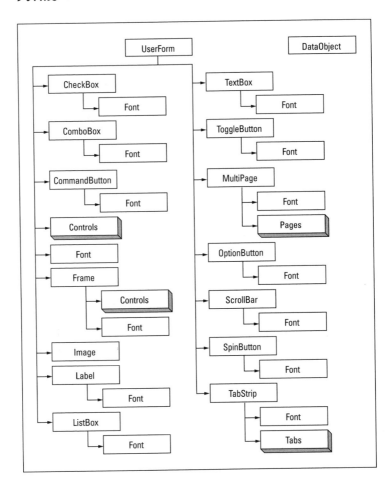

VB Editor

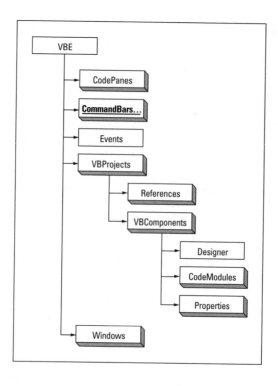

Techie Talk

ActiveX: An umbrella term that refers to a group of Microsoft technologies that enable applications and application components to communicate and interoperate with each other. Many of these same technologies were once known by the term OLE.

ANSI: The *ANSI* (*American National Standards Institute*) character set uses single-byte characters which means it can only represent 256-different characters unlike the *Unicode* character set.

argument: An argument is one of the items you must pass to a VBA procedure in order to call the procedure. The creator of the procedure determines the arguments you must pass. Sometimes an argument is *optional,* which means you don't have to complete it.

array: A set of variables that can be treated at times as if they were one. You access individual elements of an array by using the array's *index*. For example, the array `Friends( )` may contain the names of all your friends, whereas the element `varFriends(14)` may contain the name of your friend Joan Kunzinger.

Automation: A technology that enables you to *automate* (or control) one application (the Automation *server*) from another (the Automation *controller*). Automation is also called ActiveX Automation and was previously known as OLE Automation.

break mode: A state in which your executing VBA code pauses. This mode allows you to *single step* (execute the code one line at a time) through your code, examine variables in the *Locals window,* check the value of custom *watch* expressions in the *Watches window,* and use the *Immediate window* to evaluate expressions or modify your code.

breakpoint: A statement in your code where you've indicated you want VBA to pause execution.

character system: In some locales, such as Asia, characters cannot be represented by a single-byte character system (SBCS), which normally represents Latin-based languages. Thus, a double-byte character system (DBCS) must represent such characters.

class: A template for a custom *object.* You define a class by using a special type of *module* called a *class module.* You use a class to create your own *objects* that behave much like VBA and host application objects.

class module: A special type of module you use to define a *class.*

collection: A named list of items to which you can add, delete, and retrieve items.

compile: The process whereby code gets translated from what you type — the source code — to a form that VBA can execute — p-code.

compiler directive: A special instruction to the VBA compiler that is evaluated by the compiler as it compiles the code.

concatenate: When you concatenate two strings, you splice them together. For example, `"red"` concatenated with `"cup"` becomes `"redcup"`. There are two concatenation operators in VBA: & and +.

constant: A named location in memory that stores a value that can't change as the program executes.

data type: A specific type of *variable* that can hold values that meet certain rules. For example, an `Integer` variable can hold whole numbers between -32768 and +32767 but can't hold strings or decimal values. The special *Variant* data type can hold any other type of data.

date/time value: To efficiently support date arithmetic, VBA internally stores dates and times as the number of days (and fractional days) since December 30, 1899.

DLL: A DLL (*dynamic link library*) is a compiled external library of procedures that's available to any Windows application.

empty: A special uninitialized state of a *Variant* variable. Variants are `Empty` before you initialize them by placing a value into them. You can also make a variable `Empty` by setting it equal to the `Empty` keyword.

error trap: A section of a procedure that VBA jumps to when a run-time error occurs. You indicate to VBA that it should redirect errors to your trap (also known as an *error handler*) by using the `On Error GoTo` statement.

event: A change in the state of your VBA program or the host application that you can react to. For example, a VBA User Form triggers the VBA program's `Initialize` event when the form loads. You react to events by specifying a piece of code called an *event procedure* that hooks into the event.

event procedure: A procedure that is called when a matching *event* is triggered.

event sink: A variable you can define in a *class module* (using the `WithEvents` keyword) to tell a program you want to be notified when certain events occur in other objects. This allows you to define *event procedures* that react to the events of these objects.

file access mode: When you open a file using VBA's `Open` statement, you must choose a file access mode, which can be *Append, Binary, Input, Output,* or *Random.*

file number: When you create or open a file using the VBA file keywords, you must refer to the open file using the file's file number — a unique number between 1 and 511.

function: A function is type of *procedure* that returns a value to the calling procedure.

hexadecimal: A number represented using base 16, where each digit can range from 0 to F.

host: The application program such as Microsoft Access, or Visio where VBA is running. VBA is like a parasite (a good parasite): It can't live on it's own — an application of some sort must host it.

IDE: IDE stands for *integrated development environment.* This is the editor you use to create your VBA programs. The VBA IDE includes lots of cool features that make it easy to enter, edit, debug, and manage your code.

Immediate window: The *Immediate window* is a window in the VBA IDE where you can test VBA procedures, evaluate expressions, and change the values of variables while your code is in break mode.

instantiate: Before you can use most *objects,* you must first create or instantiate the object. Some built-in objects are already instantiated by VBA or the *host* application.

IntelliSense: A set of features built into the VBA IDE that can make programming easier. If enabled (choose Tools⇨Options), IntelliSense displays — as you type — a summary of a keyword's definition and a list of constants for its arguments. IntelliSense also displays a list of the properties and methods of objects.

Locals window: The *Locals window* is a window in the VBA IDE you can use while in *break mode* to lookup the value of program variables as well as the values of various properties of objects.

Me: A built-in object variable that refers to the class or form (and in Microsoft Access, the report) from which the code is currently executing.

method: A *method* is an action an object can perform. VBA's built-in objects and host application objects have methods. For example, the VBA collection object has the `Add` method. You can also define methods for class module objects by creating `Public` functions and subs in the class modules.

module: A group of related *procedures* that you tell VBA to keep together as a unit.

null: A special "unknown" state of a `Variant` variable. You can make a variable `Null` by setting it equal to the `Null` keyword. You can determine if a variable is `Null` by using the `IsNull` function.

object: A thing that has *properties* and *methods* (and may contain collections of other things) that you can manipulate using code. VBA contains several built-in objects such as *collection* objects and the Debug object (an object that represents the *Immediate* window). VBA *host* programs contain additional objects. To create your own objects, you must first create a *class module*.

object model: A schematic diagram that represents the relationships between an application's objects. For example, by consulting the Microsoft Word object model, you can learn that `Document` objects contain (among other things) `Shape` objects.

octal: A number represented using base 8, where each digit can range from 0 to 7.

parameter: When you create a procedure, you determine which parameters the procedure will accept. Parameters and *return values* allow your procedure to communicate with a calling procedure. When a calling procedure calls your procedure, it passes *arguments* that match each of your parameters. You may declare some parameters as optional.

procedure: The smallest unit of executable VBA code. A procedure begins with a `Function`, `Sub`, or `Property` procedure statement and ends with an `End Function`, `End Sub`, or `End Property` statement.

property: A property is an attribute of an *object* that you retrieve and/or set. VBA's built-in objects and host application objects have properties. For example, the VBA collection object has the `count` property. You can also define properties for `class module` objects using `Property` procedures.

registry: A special operating system database that stores and retrieves various settings in a hierarchy of *keys* (also sometimes called *nodes*).

return value: The value returned by a function. For example, you might call the VBA UCase function by using code like this: `strName = UCase("geoff")`. In this case, UCase's return value would be "GEOFF".

static: A variable is said to be *static* if it retains its value between calls to the procedure in which it lives.

subroutine: A subroutine is a type of procedure that doesn't return a value to the calling procedure.

twip: A screen-independent unit of measurement equal to 1/20 of a printer's point. There are approximately 1,440 twips to a logical inch or 567 twips to a logical centimeter.

Unicode: In contrast to the *ANSI* one-byte character set which can only represent 256 different characters, the Unicode character set, which uses two-byte characters, can hold up to 65536 characters. This means that it can more easily represent languages that contain more than 256 characters.

User Form: VBA allows you to create forms, called *User Forms* (or *Microsoft forms*) to present and/or capture data from users.

user-defined type: A custom data type you define using a `Type` statement. A user-defined type contains one or more elements which must be made up of existing data types.

variable: A named location in memory that stores a value that changes during program execution.

variant: A special type of variable that can contain any other data type: numbers, strings, arrays, dates, even objects.

VBA: *VBA* stands for Visual Basic for Applications. The programming language used in Microsoft Office and other products such as Visio and Crystal Reports. A dialect of the BASIC (*Beginner's All-Purpose Symbolic Instruction Code*) language, which was invented in 1964 at Dartmouth College. An easy-to-learn and easy-to-use, yet powerful, programming language.

watch: A variable or expression in your code that you can examine, and even change, as your code executes. You can use the *Locals window* to view the value of any variable used in your code, or create custom watch expressions using the *Watches window*.

Watches window: When you create custom watch expressions in VBA, they are placed in this window, which you can use to view their contents.

zero-length string: A string with zero length, often indicated using " ".

Index

K

L

Q

R

IDG BOOKS WORLDWIDE REGISTRATION CARD

RETURN THIS REGISTRATION CARD FOR FREE CATALOG

Title of this book: VBA For Dummies® Quick Reference

My overall rating of this book: ❑ Very good [1] ❑ Good [2] ❑ Satisfactory [3] ❑ Fair [4] ❑ Poor [5]

How I first heard about this book:

❑ Found in bookstore; name: [6]

❑ Advertisement: [8]

❑ Word of mouth; heard about book from friend, co-worker, etc.: [10]

❑ Book review: [7]

❑ Catalog: [9]

❑ Other: [11]

What I liked most about this book:

What I would change, add, delete, etc., in future editions of this book:

Other comments:

Number of computer books I purchase in a year: ❑ 1 [12] ❑ 2-5 [13] ❑ 6-10 [14] ❑ More than 10 [15]

I would characterize my computer skills as: ❑ Beginner [16] ❑ Intermediate [17] ❑ Advanced [18] ❑ Professional [19]

I use ❑ DOS [20] ❑ Windows [21] ❑ OS/2 [22] ❑ Unix [23] ❑ Macintosh [24] ❑ Other: [25]_____ (please specify)

I would be interested in new books on the following subjects:
(please check all that apply, and use the spaces provided to identify specific software)

❑ Word processing: [26]

❑ Data bases: [28]

❑ File Utilities: [30]

❑ Networking: [32]

❑ Other: [34]

❑ Spreadsheets: [27]

❑ Desktop publishing: [29]

❑ Money management: [31]

❑ Programming languages: [33]

I use a PC at (please check all that apply): ❑ home [35] ❑ work [36] ❑ school [37] ❑ other: [38]

The disks I prefer to use are ❑ 5.25 [39] ❑ 3.5 [40] ❑ other: [41]

I have a CD ROM: ❑ yes [42] ❑ no [43]

I plan to buy or upgrade computer hardware this year: ❑ yes [44] ❑ no [45]

I plan to buy or upgrade computer software this year: ❑ yes [46] ❑ no [47]

Name: _____ Business title: [48]

Type of Business: [49]

Address (❑ home [50] ❑ work [51]/Company name: _____)

Street/Suite#

City [52]/State [53]/Zipcode [54]: _____ Country [55]

❑ **I liked this book!**
You may quote me by name in future IDG Books Worldwide promotional materials.

My daytime phone number is _____

IDG BOOKS
THE WORLD OF COMPUTER KNOWLEDGE

❏ YES!

Please keep me informed about IDG's World of Computer Knowledge. Send me the latest IDG Books catalog.

NO POSTAGE
NECESSARY
IF MAILED
IN THE
UNITED STATES

BUSINESS REPLY MAIL
FIRST CLASS MAIL   PERMIT NO. 2605   FOSTER CITY, CALIFORNIA

IDG Books Worldwide
919 E Hillsdale Blvd, STE 400
Foster City, CA 94404-9691

ll₁l₁₁₁l₁₁l₁l₁₁lll₁₁₁₁l₁₁ll₁l₁₁₁ll₁₁l₁l₁₁₁₁ll₁l₁₁ll